Gram & Gran Save the Summer

Stephen Chiger & Daniel Pereira

Illustrated by Louis Decrevel

Praise for Gram and Gran

"Put together the wordplay of *The Phantom Tollbooth*, the imagination of *Willie Wonka and the Chocolate Factory*, and the problem-solving mysteries of *Encyclopedia Brown*, make it about media and digital literacy, and you've got *Gran and Gram Save the Summer*. Now, when someone asks what it means to teach media literacy from a place of curiosity and discovery instead of anxiety and fear, I can point to this book and say, 'Like this.'… This book is a must-have for every middle-grade library."

– Faith Rogow, author, *Media Literacy for Young Children: Teaching Beyond the Screen Time Debates*

"Attention media literacy teachers! Here's a clever, imaginative, and much-needed guidebook, cleverly disguised as a whimsical fantasy, that helps middle school kids learn to suss out and avoid online misinformation, scams, and phonies. It will give them the critical thinking skills needed to navigate our chaotic online universe."

– Sam Swope, founder and president, The Academy for Teachers

"Stephen and Dan have created a thoroughly original, relevant work that not only encourages critical thinking but demonstrates how digital literacy skills are necessary in almost every aspect of life. In an entertaining way and engaging way, they've provided readers with tools to help them navigate the digital world. I wish this book had existed when my sons were younger."

– Julie Smith, author, *Master the Media: How Teaching Media Can Save Our Plugged-In World*

"Today's readers are tomorrow's leaders. And for years to come, they'll remember how *Gram and Gran* taught them to check sources, question authority, and find the best [extra crispy bacon-jalapeno-cheddar-gorgonzola] poppers in town. *Gram and Gran Save the Summer* is *The Phantom Tollbooth* for kids raised in digital playgrounds—and it couldn't be more needed."

– Aldalyn Eleanor Ross, children's librarian, Newark Public Library

"*Gram and Gran Save the Summer* introduces media literacy in a fresh and engaging way, weaving essential skills seamlessly into an exciting narrative. By tackling important topics head-on, readers gain the tools to navigate today's media landscape with confidence and critical thinking."

– Brittany Washburn, Technology Curriculum Developer, brittanywashburn.com

"*Gram and Gran* is such a clever and delightful way to impart media literacy skills. Children are sure to love it—and parents and teachers too – since it invites the kinds of conversations we want and need."

– Barbara Martinez, former investigative reporter, *The Wall Street Journal*

Gram and Gran Save the Summer

©2024 by Stephen Chiger and Daniel Pereira

All rights reserved. No part of this publication may be reproduced in any form or by any means—electronic, photocopying, recording, or mechanical means, including information storage and retrieval systems without the permission in writing from the publisher, except by a reviewer who may quote brief passages in a review. For more information regarding permission, contact the publisher at publishing@teachergoals.com. For bulk purchases, go to teachergoals.com/bulk.

Published by TeacherGoals Publishing, LLC, Beech Grove, IN

www.teachergoals.com

Cover Design & Illustrations by: Louis Decrevel

Interior Design by: Heather Brown

Edited by: Lois Budesheim

Copy Edited by: Carrie Turner and Andrew Sobel

Library of Congress Control Number: 2024934767

Paperback ISBN: 978-1-959419-18-1

ASIN: B0CW19FKNR

First Printing: April 2024

Dedication

To Rosemary and Cole

Introducing...

Deja   D'Angelo   Nia

Phineas Paperplate

Gram & Gran

The PII Kids

Ruthbert Rugglesford

Table of Contents

Chapter 1: Gram and Gran 1

Chapter 2: So They Say 18

Chapter 3: The Museum of the Misunderstood 42

Chapter 4: The Reviews Are In... 64

Chapter 5: Gran's Special Medicine... 82

Chapter 6: Reliable Sources... 101

Chapter 7: Gone Phishing 125

Chapter 8: Cherry Picking 138

Chapter 9: Conspiracies A Go-Go... 154

Chapter 10: Pure Puffery... 184

Chapter 11: Gram and Gran Save the Summer,
          and Also Probably the World 210

Chapter 1: Gram and Gran

The two worst words Nia could think of were "family" and "meeting."

Actually, "family" wasn't too bad, usually. And meetings were boring, but boring stuff was just part of life. The problem was when you put them together. The phrase "family meeting" always meant trouble.

It was at a family meeting that Mom told her they were going to move from the only home she had known to a brownstone in a city where they knew no one. It was at a family meeting that Nia and her younger brother, D'Angelo, learned that their first cat, Boo-Boo Kitty, had gone across the Rainbow Bridge to Pet Heaven. It was even at a family meeting that Mom told them they would be adopting a new baby sister, Deja. That one hadn't turned out so bad, now that Deja was seven, but when she had been a baby and couldn't do anything but spit up and cry in the middle of the night, it had been pretty rough.

And now, here it was again: Mom had called a family

meeting for this evening, just three days before summer break was going to begin.

"So…" Mom said, taking a deep breath once they had gathered on the living room couch. "I know you were all looking forward to going to Camp Wildwood this summer, but I got a call from the director today. You know that forest fire that's been burning up there? Well, it's getting too close to the camp. The forest service is making them close until it gets under control. It could be a couple of weeks."

Nia glanced at her siblings. Deja was looking at Mom with a sleepy look, as if she'd been woken up too fast and couldn't quite believe a dream was over. D'Angelo, on the other hand, was grinning a mile wide.

"YES!" he pumped his fist. "Thank you, forest fire!"

Nia frowned. "What's wrong with you, D? We were going to have a great time there."

"Maybe *you* were, Ms. Counselor-In-Training. But eight weeks with no internet, no phones, and no screens? Forget that! Summer here is gonna be so much bet—"

"Hold on, D'Angelo," Mom interrupted. "I've got that assignment in Beijing. This is a huge opportunity for me—for all of us. I can't stay home with you." Mom's voice had a ring of finality. She'd already done the work of convincing herself.

"So we're going to Beijing?" asked Deja, her eyes lighting up.

"No, honey. Actually, you're…" Mom paused as if she

were unsure what she was going to say next. Then her words came out in a tumble. "I'm sending you to stay with my parents for the summer."

The children were silent. Then they erupted.

"But we've hardly even *met* them!" cried Nia.

"Yeah. Just postcards and phone calls. Where do they even *live*?" asked D'Angelo.

"Yay!" shouted Deja.

"Calm down, people! One at a time. Now, you know, when I was growing up, and for a long time afterward, your Gram and Gran weren't always...reliable. But a couple of years ago, they settled down, and we've been talking weekly ever since. They always remember your birthdays, and they always ask to speak to you. They're not strangers."

"Why didn't you tell us?" asked Nia.

"I wanted to make sure that they'd really and truly become more reliable, and they have. They're still...different...than most people, but I have no doubt you'll be safe with them, and it's past time for you to meet. They're excited to get to know you."

"You'll be perfectly safe," she said a second time. "And best of all, they live in a little town called Barnaby's Corner off the coast of Maine, far away, just like camp would have been. There probably isn't even a cell phone signal there. You'll have a screen-free summer."

Mom said that last sentence with an air of self-satisfaction.

She was always asking her kids to peel their faces away from their screens for a minute, and usually they did when they weren't too deep into whatever they were doing. It's not that they were rude—far from it, in fact. It's just that Mom had said it so many times. Her words had begun to fade into the background like a tacky yellow wallpaper.

Now it looked like she was finally going to get what she wanted.

* * *

Three days later, they were on a train bound for Barnaby's Cape, or Cove, or whatever the island was called. Nia sat in the window seat, frowning at the fields and towns passing by. They were already in Maine, less than an hour away from their stop. With every mile, a knot in her stomach was growing bigger and bigger.

D'Angelo was sitting next to her. He nudged her with his elbow. She looked at him. On his other side was Deja, fast asleep, her head against his shoulder. D'Angelo looked at Deja meaningfully and then back at Nia.

He whispered, "So, what do you think the *real* deal is with Gram and Gran?"

That was what their grandparents had called themselves in each of the postcards and birthday cards they had sent over the years: notes from all over the world, messages attached to trinkets from here and there. The cards were brief, interesting, and impersonal, full of vivid details that painted a picture of where they were but not who they were. A typical one went something like:

> *"Greetings from Tangiers, Morocco! The weather is hot, but we're enjoying mint tea and tangerines (Did you know tangerines were named for Tangiers?) and staying in the shade. Enclosed, please find some little tokens of our affection. We picked them up in a local market. With copious love, Gran and Gram."*

Nia sighed. "What do you mean, D?"

"I *mean*..." he shot back, "did you hear how Mom said we'd be safe with them *twice*?"

"Right. Because we'll be safe with them."

"C'mon Nia, think. When you go to the doctor and they say the needle's not going to hurt, what does that mean?"

"It means it's going to hurt."

"*Exactly.*"

"Mom's not a nurse. She's a journalist."

"Don't be so gullible," D'Angelo said, rolling his eyes. "I bet they're criminals. Big time. They've probably been on the run all these years."

"Who's criminals?" asked a sleepy voice. Deja was awake.

Nia glared at D'Angelo. "*Nobody's* criminals."

"Oh," said Deja. She seemed a little disappointed to hear it.

* * *

"I think you're really going to enjoy your stay in Barnaby's Corner. Your mom told me about what happened to your camp, but hopefully your summer here will be just as fun," said Phineas T. Paperplate, the local newspaper editor. Mom and Phineas went way back. They had been in journalism school together and then worked on the same paper when Nia was little, before D'Angelo and Deja were born. Mom and Phineas had kept in touch ever since, as journalists often did. So when Mom realized that he and her parents lived in the same town, she'd asked Phineas to pick them up at the station. He was now in the process of sailing them—in a periwinkle blue tugboat—to an island well off the coast.

"You'll love Phineas," she had said. "He's a great guy and one of the most honest people I know. You can always trust him."

"How about Gram and Gran?" D'Angelo had asked. "Can't we trust *them*?"

"You can trust them for the big stuff, like keeping you safe and fed and loved. For the small stuff, you're going to have to figure it out for yourself," Mom had replied cryptically. "That's what I did. It's probably why I became a journalist."

Mr. Paperplate had been the editor of the local paper for a decade, and he looked just like the children imagined a newspaper editor would. He was tall and thin with salt-and-pepper hair topped by an old-timey fedora. He had a keen, inquisitive look and a mustache that commanded respect.

"Do you wear that hat because you work for a newspaper?" Deja asked him.

"Oh, no, sweetie. I wear it because I have *style*." Phineas's mustache lifted slightly to reveal a grin.

D'Angelo was unimpressed. "Couldn't Gram and Gran come get us?" he asked, his eyes fixed on the vanishing coastline.

"I suppose so," said Phineas. "But the space between *can* and *should* is so wide you could drive a truck through it. Or a tugboat, in this case, I suppose. The last time Gram and Gran drove a boat, it took the Coast Guard a whole hour to catch them."

Phineas paused. Here he was, an ambassador for the town, and he wanted to make a good impression. "Your Gram is known for having excellent gardening skills," he added. "And Gran is the pitcher for the town softball team. Gran's a southpaw, like me." Phineas wiggled the fingers on his left hand.

In addition to being the newspaper editor, Phineas T. Paperplate was the town's only taxi driver, the curator of its local museum, and its backup tugboat captain. "There's not a lot of news in Barnaby's Corner unless you go looking for it," he explained. "The other stuff helps me keep my nose to the ground."

"Why?" asked Deja. "What's on the ground?"

"It's a figure of speech," Nia explained. "It means he

pays close attention to what's going on."

"Sure does, and speaking of attention, if you look starboard, you'll see something worth paying attention to." He wrinkled his nose and nodded off to the right.

It was a bright but hazy day. Far in the distance, the children could see a tall—an impossibly tall—structure pointing into the air, like a lone finger hailing a taxi.

"Wow! What *is* that?" shouted Deja.

"Keep looking," replied Phineas.

As they got closer, they could see the scene more clearly. From the side, the island looked a bit like a pot belly rising from the sea, as though a sleeping giant was floating on his back, his tummy bulging in the sun. *Who would think to build houses on a place like this?* thought Nia.

In most ways, Barnaby's Corner looked like a typical sleepy island town, all shops and cottages and narrow streets winding their way up the hill. But jutting from the center was something fantastic, a seventy-seven-story high-rise topped by a one-hundred-foot antenna. Nia's jaw dropped.

"Ah, yes. Some brief history," said Phineas. "That tower was built by our founder, Barnaby Babel. Brilliant man, that one was. Too bad about the disappearance. It's still unsolved, you know."

"Wait," said D'Angelo. "What?"

"Babel's Tower? He never gave it a name, so we just call it the Tower. You see, Mr. Babel was ahead of his time. He founded our town to give everyone access to all parts of the internet. Gave away all the land except for the Tower, too. Believed it was the future, and he was right. Because of the Tower, we never lose signal, and we never have to charge anything."

"I think D was wondering why Mr. Babel disappeared," Deja said.

"No one knows. But that was decades ago. Like he was blinked out of existence. Of course, the newspaper did an exhaustive search, but we couldn't turn up a thing. But every year, on New Year's Day, a huge deposit is made in a special bank account 'for maintenance and upgrading of the Tower.' So even though the Tower was built years ago, it's always state of the art. But that's a mystery for another day. For now, let's get you to that tower so you can see it up close. It's where your Gram and Gran live, after all."

Up close, the Tower was even more astonishing than from a distance. It was an obnoxious shade of green, something Nia had never seen before and hoped to never see again. But it shimmered as though it were alive. And out front, grinning from ear to ear, were Gram and Gran.

"Ho, Gran! Ho, Gram!" said Phineas as he set down the luggage. "Well, I should get going. You've all got catching up to do. If you ever need me, just give me a call."

"What number should we use?" asked Nia.

"People just call me Mr. Paperplate, but I've always fancied the number four," he said, heading off before Nia could reply. She grabbed Deja's hand a bit more tightly than usual. They were most definitely a long way from home.

* * *

"Welcome, children!" said the couple standing in front of the great green skyscraper. They both had a kindly look about them, which put the children a bit more at ease.

"I'm sure it has been a long trip," said the man, extending his left hand to give each of them a firm handshake.

His grip is surprisingly strong considering how wrinkly his hands look, thought Nia.

"You must be tired from all that traveling. You probably want to rest," said the woman, hugging each child ten seconds longer than felt necessary. "I think that's why your mother sent you here, for a good long break away from that

sleepy city of yours. Not enough noise out that way, I always tell her. Too quiet."

"More like to keep us away from technology," said D'Angelo under his breath, catching eyes from his older sister for the comment.

"But, child, why would she *ever* want to do that?" asked the woman. She was broad but not heavy. Her dark skin contrasted nicely with her white hair, which she styled in a fishtail that draped over her shoulder.

"Yes," said the man. "We *love* technology. Didn't your mom tell you? That's why we settled down here! Though, come to think of it, she was too busy taking care of the three of you to come visit. I'll admit it's a bit of a trip." He was taller than the woman, but not by much, and he was white and very skinny. His head was crowned with a few wisps of hair, combed over in memory of what was once—the children assumed—much more than what he currently had.

"But there'll be time for all of that later. Why don't you kids follow Gran up to your rooms?" asked the woman.

"Yes, you should follow Gran," said the man.

"Wait," said Deja. "I'm confused. Which one of you is which?"

"I am!" said both people simultaneously.

"That's Gran!" they said, pointing to the other.

"And I'm Gram," they said again in unison.

"Gran is short for Gra*n*dma," said the woman, emphasizing the *n* sound.

"No, no, I believe it's short for Gra*n*dpa," said the man, adding stress to the *n* as well.

"Gram is clearly short for Gra*m*-pa," said the woman.

"Oh, no. I quite think it's a quick way to say Gra*m*-ma," replied the man.

"Well, we can't both be Gran. I suppose we've forgotten again," said the woman with a twinkle in her eye. And with that, the two began to titter back and forth as though the children weren't even there. This went on for a bit. Say what you would about Gram and Gran's quirks—it was clear they were very much smitten with each other and were quite possibly having some fun at the children's expense.

D'Angelo sighed. It had been a long day, and he was fresh out of patience. "You've got to be kidding!"

Gram and Gran looked up.

"Oh, child, we're always kidding," said the one. "But we're always serious about it," followed the other.

"Here, we'll make this easy since you're clearly tired. Why don't you ask us a question to figure out who's who, something only one of us would know?"

Nia and her siblings fell into a huddle. This was all a bit ridiculous, but if they were going to get along, they'd need to play Gram and Gran's game.

"I've got it," said Deja. "I know Gram loves to garden. Which one of you is the gardener?"

"I am," said the man. "But I am too," said the woman. "We both garden. In fact, you can see our flowers right there in front of the Tower. Only one of us wins awards for it, though."

"Ugh," said Nia. "That didn't get us anywhere."

"Seriously? This is ridicul—" D'Angelo stopped short as he surveyed the flower beds in front of the Tower. Lying in one of them was a softball. D'Angelo smiled. He had a plan to solve this riddle and get some rest. "Since you're both gardeners, I'm sure you'll want to pick up that softball that rolled into the flowerbed."

"Oh, goodness!" the woman said, and scooped up the ball.

"Mind tossing it this way?" D'Angelo asked. The woman wound back her right arm and lobbed him a direct pitch. He caught it midair.

It was the last clue he needed...

D'Angelo figured out a way to tell who's who. Can you?

Review what you've learned about Gram and Gran, and then turn the page for a hint if you need it.

Hint from D'Angelo

Sometimes people are fibbing, and it can be hard to tell. Deja asked a broad question, which made it easy for both Gram and Gran to answer. One thing she could do is ask a specific question about gardening, something only an expert would know the answer to. The problem is, if Gram and Gran decide to fib, we won't know enough to catch them unless we know a lot about gardening, too.

If we're going to figure out who is trying to trick us, we'll need to be just as clever as they are. So it helps to consider what you know or can learn from reliable sources, like Mr. Paperplate. Reliable sources are **credible** (another word for trustworthy): like Mr. Paperplate, they have a track record of getting things right or correcting their mistakes when they make them. We can use what we know from **reliable sources** to check the claims that other people make.

How can we use outside information to help us know who is really Gran? Think back to what you learned from Mr. Paperplate about Gram and Gran, then to the things you saw them say and do. Oh, and if there are any words here you didn't know, go check them out.

Conclusion: Will the Real Gram and Gran Please Stand Up?

"So did Gran throw the ball?" wondered Deja. "I know Gran is good at softball."

"Gran is," said D'Angelo, "but that's Gram. Mr. Paperplate said Gran is a *southpaw*, and that means he's left-handed. So Gram is short for Grandma and Gran is short for Grandpa. I knew it when I thought back to those handshakes. Gran used his *left* hand, while most people use their right."

"Well, I'll be," Gran said with a toothy smile. "Looks like I'm showing the kids to their rooms. Thanks for that reminder." None of the children could fully tell whether he was kidding or serious. "Grab those bags and head for the elevator, kids. Gram and I live pretty high up."

"How high?" asked Nia.

But Gran just winked.

"Don't be coy, Gran," said Gram. "Our apartment is at the all-the-way, very-very, absolute tippy top of the Tower—or what you folks would call the penthouse."

Chapter 2: So They Say

"Orr-orr-roo!"

Deja rubbed her eyes. Was everything that happened yesterday real? Did her Gram and Gran live at the top of a tower

on a strange little island? What would have caused the owner to vanish?

And. Why. Was. There. A. Rooster. In. Her. Bed?!?!

"Heya, kiddo!" said Gram with a voice far too cheerful for so early in the morning. "Don't mind Mr. Cock-a-Doo. We just borrowed him from our rooftop chicken farm to help you get up. You know what They say: *Early to bed, and early to rise, makes a grandchild healthy, wealthy, and wise.*"

Deja was still half-asleep. There was no way Gram and Gran were raising chickens on the roof. No way. But, come to think of it, she had heard something about "early to bed and early to rise." Still, surely an alarm clock would have worked.

"Your siblings are already in the kitchen. Gran is making his famous chocolate pancakes."

The most delicious aroma tickled Deja's nose. She could forget about the rooster if breakfast was about to taste as good as it smelled.

"This is one of Gran's specialties. He's a whiz with any food that mostly comes from a box."

Deja wasn't sure if Gram meant that as a compliment or not. There was something about the way she spoke that made it hard to tell if she was joking. But some of Deja's favorite foods—brownies, cereal, and mac and cheese—came from boxes. That last one had landed her in trouble since Mom's mac and cheese was a closely guarded family secret and a Big Deal at holidays. But Deja reasoned that that dish was entirely different from the yellow, powdered cheese Nia would make for her in the winter when Mom was busy. Deja looked guiltily at Gram, who had been talking this whole time while she daydreamed.

"...thinks he's clever, but I know the secret ingredient. It's chocolate, and I for one—"

"Aaaah-choo!" Deja sneezed a swift and single time, sending a handful of Mr. Cock-a-Doo's feathers off the bed and dancing into the air.

"Oh, no!" cried Gram. "Sounds like you may have a sniffle. Let's bundle you up."

"It's not a cold. It's allergies," said Deja. She still had uncomfortable memories of her first-grade class's trip to the petting zoo. Her friends all got to touch sheep and cows, while all Deja got to do was rub her eyes red.

But Gram would hear none of it. Seemingly out of thin air, she conjured a wool cap and scarf and was wrapping Deja up like some sort of fuzzy wintertime mummy.

"Gram! It's summer!"

"Oh, I know that, child," Gram said as she pulled an inch-thick wool hat over Deja's ears. "But you know what They say: *Get bundled up so you don't catch a cold.* A lot of people seem to only remember this in December, but if you can catch a chill then, who's to say you can't catch it any time? That's probably why folks catch summer colds."

Deja paused again. She did remember her mom bundling her up last winter. And even though she was sure the sneeze was a symptom of her allergies, she didn't want to catch a cold. Gram's logic checked out, even if it did feel a little off-kilter.

At the breakfast table, D'Angelo and Nia couldn't stop laughing at the bundled-up Deja.

"You gonna build a snowman?" asked D'Angelo.

"Awww, I think she looks cute," said Nia, snapping a picture for later.

Deja did not appreciate that one bit. "They say you should bundle up to prevent a cold. Gram *told* me."

"She sure did," laughed D'Angelo, who had far less faith in authorities than either of his sisters. For him, this was just another example of why you couldn't trust anyone but yourself.

"I solved that problem lickety-split," smiled Gram. "You know what They say: *There's no time like the present.*"

Gran got a mischievous look about him. "But maybe you shouldn't have rushed, Gram. You know what They also say: *Fools rush in where angels fear to tread.* It's bad to move too quickly."

Gram was ready with a comeback. "Yes, but They say that *she who hesitates is lost*, Gran."

"Oh, Gram. But in addition, They say: *You should look before you leap.*"

And with that, the two began tittering about again, very much as though the children weren't there at all.

* * *

Breakfast was finished. Well, at least breakfast was finished for Gram, Gran, Nia, and D'Angelo. For Deja, breakfast was a nightmare that refused to end. Halfway through the meal, Gram had added a snowsuit to Deja's outfit. "They say *you can never be too careful*," Gram had explained. The snowsuit was puffy and stiff and made Deja's arms stick out from her sides so that she could barely get them in front of her to use her fork and knife. Each bite required her full concentration, and even then, getting the food in her mouth was not a guarantee.

"Gram and Gran, can we go see the town? I bet there's all sorts of cool stuff there," Nia said as Deja continued to struggle with the pancakes.

"No problem," Gran said. "Barnaby's Corner is a nice,

safe place. That's one of the reasons we settled here. I think you kids can manage to explore on your own. And if you ever get lost, just look for the Tower and head towards it. You can't miss it."

"Awesome!" said D'Angelo. Mom had let him and Nia go out on their own at home in Brooklyn sometimes, but every time she did it, she sounded like she was trying desperately not to panic. It always made him nervous, like maybe there *was* something to be worried about. But Gran seemed totally unconcerned like he thought the kids could handle themselves. That was a new feeling, and it suited D'Angelo just fine.

Gram agreed with Gran. "But I think Deja had better stay here with us," she added. "It's hot today and she'll overheat outside. And besides, *three's a crowd*, as They say."

Deja wailed. "That's not fair! Besides, if I stay here, then there will be three people *here*."

Gran patted her on the shoulder sympathetically. "Don't worry about that. You know what They say: *The more the merrier*. You, Gram, and I will have a great time here. We're going to have a guest dropping by later, so there'll be lots to do."

Deja shot a desperate glance at Nia. Nia knew exactly what the look was saying: *You have to speak up and fix this! It's not fair! I want to go too.* Nia grimaced. She knew that Deja was right. It wasn't fair. And she knew that sisters needed to stick together. But…there was a whole town to explore, and she had to admit that having a seven year old along could really cramp her style. She looked away from Deja and gulped.

"Great!" she said. "Thanks Gram and Gran! We'll be back before dinner time. Have a nice day, Deja. We'll—"

She froze when she saw the look of absolute betrayal that Deja was giving her.

She cleared her throat. "Don't worry, I promise we'll keep you in the loop, Day. You can borrow Gram's tablet. I'll text pictures and descriptions and everything! It'll be almost like you're there with us. And I *promise* you and I can go out another day and explore, just the two of us." She knew that D'Angelo wouldn't mind being left alone later. He could lose himself for hours reading about Bigfoot or the moon landing or some other weird conspiracy.

Already imaptient, D'Angelo cried, "Let's go!" He and Nia got up from the table and hurried out to the door. As it closed behind them, Nia could almost feel Deja's eyes burning a hole in the back of her head.

* * *

"Ever wonder why apartment building floors all look alike?" D'Angelo said, raising an eyebrow at Nia. "It's like they WANT you to get lost. Like they're HIDING something."

Normally, Nia would have had a snappy reply, but they had promised to drop off some of Gram's zucchini marmalade to the neighbor in 32B, so she went along with it. And, to D'Angelo's point, 32B did look like every other apartment in the building from the outside.

The inside was a different matter altogether. It was filled, top to bottom, with all kinds of stuff: games and electronics and clothing and dishware and knickknacks and lots and lots of receipts from online deliveries. Most of it was unopened. Boxes piled from floor to ceiling took up the whole room except for the middle, where a trendy-looking man in brand-new sneakers stroked his beard and peered down at a small frisbee-shaped object.

"Hello?" said Nia. "We're from the penthouse. We brought your marmalade."

"Oh!" cried the man, startled. "Wonderful. You can set it down over…well, hmm…Babel3000, where should the children place the marmalade?" he asked into the air.

A few lights flashed on the frisbee, and it replied in a pleasant tone. "They may put the marmalade by the door. Also, I have ordered you more marmalade spoons. They will arrive in an hour."

"How will they arrive in an hour? We're in the middle of nowhere!" said Nia.

"Ah, but I'm a super-triple-mega-premium member," said the man. "My packages arrive by fighter jet."

"Dude—err, Mister—can you tell me what's going on?" asked D'Angelo, genuinely confused.

"I'm just about to decide what to do today!" said the man.

"Us too!" said Nia. "It's so hard."

"Well then, you're in luck! I've got the BabelHome3000 here, and it lets me ask any question I want to the internet."

The man chirped in the general direction of the disk. "Babel3000, what would I like to do today?"

"You would like to order picnic supplies and have a picnic indoors. I have ordered them, and they will arrive in twenty-two minutes."

"Oh, that sounds great! Thank you!" sighed the man with relief. "Before I moved to this island, I would get so lost in thought. But now I don't have to worry about that anymore!"

"Wait, are you letting that thing make all your decisions for you?" asked D'Angelo, eyeing the frisbee with increased concern. "Aren't you worried about that?"

"Don't see why I should be," shrugged the man. "Knowing things is hard. Why go to the trouble? Babel3000, do I enjoy having you make my decisions for me?"

"You do! Also, I have ordered three more Babel3000's in different colors. They will arrive in 317 seconds," the machine whirred back gleefully. "But now it's time for these children to go. You think they should play outside and mind their own business." The machine's tone noticeably dropped for the last two sentences, flashing a light that, to D'Angelo, looked an awful lot like a mean wink.

"Well, there you have it, children. I think you should play outside. And who am I to disagree with what I think?"

"But—" Nia was unable to finish her sentence before the door was shut in their faces.

* * *

After discussing it, Nia and D'Angelo decided that their first task outdoors was to find Phineas at the newspaper. "Good idea," D'Angelo had said, "Let's see Deja try to get mad about missing out on some dusty office." Really, though, they just weren't sure where else to go.

They knew that the office was in the direction of the docks. They kept the sea in front of them and wound their way through quiet streets with colorful wooden houses down towards the shore. "Adorable," said Nia, taking photographs as they went. "Yeah, a little TOO adorable," D'Angelo responded suspiciously, also taking photographs, just in case.

The Barnaby Star stood on Front Street, near where Nia, D'Angelo, and Deja had docked on the day Phineas Paperplate brought them to Barnaby's Corner. It was an old two-story gray clapboard building that used to be a cannery. Although it had been painted since then, faint white letters showed through from the old days. In the bright sunlight, Nia could just barely read what they had used to say: REDSTAR HERRING. The cannery's red star, at least, had not been painted over. It was now the symbol of the island's only newspaper. Nia took a quick selfie in front of the building and sent it to Deja. "*The newspaper!*" she wrote before deciding to remove the exclamation point. "*The newspaper* 😒" she wrote. *There*, she thought. *That looks boring enough.*

* * *

"im N E V E R GOING 2 4GIV U EVAR!!!!!!" Deja typed, looking at the picture of Nia squinting into the sun. Truth be told, it didn't seem like she was having *that* much fun, but it had to be better than what had been happening to her for the last few hours.

After Deja's siblings had left, things had taken a turn for the worse. Bundling her up like a polar explorer hadn't been the end of Gram and Gran's ideas for Deja. Once she had finally managed to finish breakfast, Gran had turned to her and said, "Deja, They say you'll appreciate eating more if you have to do the dishes after each meal."

So she'd had to wash all the syrupy dishes, which was NOT easy to do in a snowsuit. She was pretty sure a fork or two was now stuck to her sleeves.

And then, once she was done with that, Gran had suggested, "They say a great way to learn hand-eye coordination would be to tidy up the chicken coop."

"But Gran, I don't even know how to tidy a chicken coop."

"They say *practice makes perfect...*"

So Deja had clomped up the steps to the roof (the elevator didn't go up there), now wearing galoshes in addition to the snowsuit. Sure enough, there on the roof, under the shadow of the antenna, was a large chicken coop full of lively, squawking chickens. A ridiculous fluffy white hen approached the wire and looked at her with a cocked eye. It was clearly thinking that it had never seen a creature like her before. Deja had to admit to herself that her outfit made her unusual. And besides, she had never seen anything quite like that chicken before either. It looked like someone had exploded a feather duster.

In the corner of the coop, there was a broom. Deja sighed and got to work.

An hour later, her chores finished, Deja collapsed on the big pink couch in the living room. Gram and Gran came in and sat down, having some tea and a talk.

"They say if you want to grow big and tall, the best approach is to sleep hanging upside down, like a bat," said Gran. The grandparents discussed this for a while and then were quiet as they sipped their tea. Deja saw an opening.

"Gram? Gran? How did you get to live in such a fancy apartment? Mom says you didn't have much money when she was young."

Gram frowned a bit. "They say *children are meant to be seen and not heard*," she said. "Or wait, is it heard but not seen?"

"Ugh!" cried Deja, feeling hot, confused, and tired. "I'm sick of hearing what *They Say*. If *They* were here, I'd ask them myself."

"Well," said Gran encouragingly. "That would be the best way to be sure! And, lucky for you, that's exactly who is stopping by this morning! Our friend will be over in a little bit, dear. We'll let you know when she gets here so you can say hi."

Deja took out Gram's tablet as she entered the bedroom. She would never forgive Nia, but she still wanted to get updates. Nothing. "*Wat r u doin now?*" she began to text, but then gave up. She wouldn't give her siblings the satisfaction of knowing she was thinking about them.

* * *

Painted on the glass were the words, "BARNABY STAR, PHINEAS T. PAPERPLATE, PUBLISHER (ALSO EDITOR, DESIGNER, COPY CHIEF, MARKETING LEAD and PAPERBOY)." Behind the windows, they could see a few desks with big, boxy old-looking computers on them in a spacious room that had probably once been the main floor of the cannery.

As they were looking around, the door opened, and Phineas stepped out, his phone to his ear, in the middle of a conversation. He noticed Nia and D'Angelo and motioned them toward him, smiling broadly. "Jane, I've got to get back to you later. I had a couple of sources stop by unexpectedly." Phineas quickly said his goodbyes to Jane and put his phone in his pocket.

"Sources?" D'Angelo asked. "Like for a newspaper article?"

Phineas grinned sheepishly. "It's easier to get off the phone with people if they think you're working on a big story. Anyway, anyone can be a source, can't they? How are you?"

"We're doing good," said Nia.

"Well, there you are. That's great information for some kind of story, I'm sure. You're sources, after all. So what brings you to the newspaper?"

"Boredom," said D'Angelo, a little too bluntly for Nia's liking.

"I guess I should show you around then! Follow me." He opened the door he had recently stepped out of and grandly motioned them in.

There was a lot less to show than Nia had expected. The room was huge, but aside from the four desks that she had seen through the window, it was sparsely decorated. They were the only people in the room.

"I present...the newsroom!" said Phineas with a bit of wilting fanfare. "Magnificent, isn't it?"

"It's...nice?" Nia tried, noticing a hint of desperation in Phineas's eyes.

"Where're the reporters?" asked D'Angelo. "And where're the big machines printing the newspapers and everything?"

But before Phineas could respond, a woman opened the newsroom door and strutted in with an air of confidence and authority. Somewhere firmly in middle age, she wore her auburn hair pulled tightly back in a ponytail, with a lavender blazer and brooch that looked positively expensive. Behind her trotted a Toy Fox Terrier, holding its head equally high and occasionally yapping in agreement with the things she said.

"Mr. Paperplate!" she pronounced. "Have you made your

decision or not?"

"Yap!" said the Toy Fox Terrier, sounding almost as demanding as its companion.

"Oh hello, Constance," stuttered Phineas. He looked at the children with a hint of panic. "Er...Nia, D'Angelo, this is Constance B. Theymselves. She has a very popular RipRap channel around these parts: a real influencer. Talks about local issues. Thousands of viewers. It's called 'I Said So'."

Constance bent down so that she was eye-to-eye with D'Angelo and Nia. "Hello, D'Angelo. Hello, Nia. It's very nice to meet you." She held out a lavender-scented hand and respectfully shook first Nia and then D'Angelo's hands. All her intensity seemed to have disappeared, but then she suddenly drew herself up to her full height as the Toy Fox Terrier began barking furiously. "My channel is called 'So *They* Say,' Mr. Paperplate. *They* is just a shorter version of my last name. Everyone knows that except, apparently, you. Now when can I start the job? I already have a hundred ideas for columns."

"Wouldn't you prefer to have this discussion in private? With the children here..." Phineas said, pushing out his hands as though he were physically trying to move the conversation away from himself.

Constance smiled warmly. "I love children," she said. "Children are some of my most loyal followers." The little dog ran over and began licking D'Angelo on the ankle. Nia had to admit: as imposing as Constance seemed to Phineas, she genuinely seemed charmed by D'Angelo and Nia.

"It's OK, Mr. Paperplate," said D'Angelo. "We can go sit on those armchairs over there."

Constance reached into an expensive-looking beaded purse and pulled out a couple of bone-shaped dog treats. She handed them to D'Angelo. "Here you go, darling. Feed these to Mr. Pickles, won't you? That's my little poopsie's name. He has his own channel, too."

D'Angelo and Nia moved to the far end of the room, Mr. Pickles bouncing behind them. Although the armchairs were quite far away from the two adults, the sound carried clearly in the large space, and Nia could hear their entire conversation while D'Angelo sat and contentedly played with the Toy Fox Terrier.

"Now then," the woman said.

"I had a look at your channel, and it's remarkable. Almost everyone in Barnaby's Corner follows you," Phineas told her.

"That's why I should have a column at the Star!" she said.

Phineas grimaced. "The thing is…I started doing some fact-checking. And none of what you say is supported by evidence."

Constance waved her hand with a perfect, stylish flick of her wrist. "I know *that*," she said. "And I respect the newspaper. I'm not asking to be a journalist. I want to write an *opinion* column."

"Yes, but the opinion articles are really supposed to be grounded in facts."

"Mr. Paperplate, have you *read* a newspaper recently? I mean, besides your own? Well, I have. I read them all. Not the news, of course, but the opinions. And that's what they are: opinions. People trust me because I simply have *exceptional* judgment. I know what I know because *I* know it. No facts needed. No facts used."

"But you have such authority when you speak! I think some people might think you *do* have the facts, even if you're just giving opinions," Phineas protested. "You just say things with confidence, and people never bother to check if they're actually correct."

"And since when was confidence a bad thing? People love my confidence. It teaches them to be more confident themselves! Besides, everyone agrees with what I'm saying. So you know it's true. That's why my channel has more viewers than your newspaper has readers." She looked down at her phone and said, "Well, just look at the time! I'm late to meet some friends. I can see you'll need to think a little more about my column. I'll come by next week, and we can discuss it."

"But…"

"Mr. Pickles! Time to go! Goodbye, Nia! Goodbye, D'Angelo! It was so nice to meet you!" At her command, the tiny dog happily rejoined her, and before Phineas or anyone else could say another word, they were out the door.

* * *

"Constance! So happy to see you!" howled Gram breathlessly as she ran to the door. "Deja, please meet Constance B. Theymselves, Barnaby Corner's very own social media star."

Constance bent down to greet Deja, just as she had done with Nia and D'Angelo earlier. "Call me *They*," she said with a wink—"everyone does, after my RipRap channel. When you hear folks talking about what '*They say*,' you can rest assured they're sharing advice from me!"

"Yap!" barked the Toy Fox Terrier in firm agreement.

Deja let out a little squeal. "He's so CUTE! What's his name? Can I pet him, Ms. Theymselves?"

"His name is Mr. Pickles, he IS cute, and yes, dear, you may pet him. And please—please!—call me *They*! It's my celebrity nickname!"

Constance B. Theymselves—or rather, "They"—was a bit of a wonder. She had an opinion on every topic, from math to psychology to psychic powers to parenting—especially parenting.

At least They convinced Gram that Deja didn't need to be bundled in the summer. "Oh, that's just for the *winter* colds," she said. "Though it's true that people lose most of their body heat through their head, so keep that hat on her if she looks chilly."

"Yap!" said Mr. Pickles, authoritatively. He began sniffing Deja's winter gear, which was already on the floor in a heap.

But then They started to share some other ideas, and many were surprising.

"You know, Deja, most people only use 10% of their brains. That means you have 90% extra brain you don't even need!"

"If you go to South America, you'll see the water spiral down the toilet counterclockwise! It's totally backwards!"

Gran and Gram were well and satisfied. Both had been relying on things They said for years. Anytime they heard a newscaster or friend say, "You know, They say that…" Gram and Gran figured they were learning something helpful. The three of them laughed over tea as Mr. Pickles ate crackers on the floor.

Deja, however, was starting to get worried. Some of the advice They gave had seemed weird:

- BEING COLD CAN MAKE YOU SICK IN WINTERTIME.
- FEED A COLD, STARVE A FEVER.
- EAT CARROTS TO IMPROVE YOUR NIGHT VISION.
- PEOPLE LOSE MOST OF THEIR BODY HEAT THROUGH THEIR HEADS.
- HUMANS USE ONLY 10% OF THEIR BRAINS.
- WATER SPIRALS THE OPPOSITE DIRECTION IN SOUTH AMERICA.

Finally, she'd had enough. She grabbed Gram's tablet

and went to her bedroom. Later that evening, she felt like she had a plan.

"Gram, can we invite your friend They over again tomorrow? I'd like to ask some questions."

Deja thinks she knows how to convince Gram and Gran to stop trusting what They say. What do you think?
How can you prove that the things They say are not necessarily credible?
Turn the page for a hint if you need it!

Hint from Deja

Gram and Gran trust what "They say" (or what "folks say," or "some people say,") because it sounds authoritative. But how do we know that what They say is true? Just because people agree on something, is that good enough? Or would we need a better source of information?

People make claims about the world all the time, but a claim is just an argument – it can be true, false, or something in between. Never rely simply on common wisdom or how confident a speaker sounds. Without facts to back them up, **claims** are mainly just a bunch of hot air. If you're not sure about what someone is saying, **ask for evidence** or proof from a **reliable source**.

Constance B. Theymselves made several claims in this chapter, and many can be investigated! If you have access to the internet, you might want to double check a few of the things Constance said (and that you've probably heard folks tell you 'They say'). Are they based on solid evidence?

Conclusion: Just Who Do They Think They Are?

Constance B. Theymselves—err, They—strutted back into Gram and Gran's apartment in very much the same manner as she had the previous day. Her blazer today was robin-egg blue, and her brooch was even larger. And right behind her was Mr. Pickles, as yappy as ever.

"Well, Gram, I always do love a visit, but I can't stay long. Mr. Pickles is doing glamor shots later this afternoon, celebrating his two-millionth follower. Anyhow, hasn't my advice answered all your questions?"

"Yap!"

Deja stepped in front of Gran. "Well..." she said. "I was wondering where you got this information."

They took a half step back and clutched at her chest in shock. "Well, I never!" They gasped.

"Deja, you've offended Constance!" shrieked Gram.

"No, no," Constance said. "It's not that at all. In point of fact, I never '*got*' this information. It's just stuff I've always known, or stuff my fellow influencers—'Folks' and 'Some People'—say. It's just content!"

D'Angelo looked up from a very interesting video he'd been watching about how the Earth was hollow. "Wait, then where do you fact-check this information?"

Deja waved her arms. "Go back to your video, D. This is mine." Nia, who heard the whole exchange, smirked a bit.

Even if Deja was still mad at her, she knew her sister wanted to show off.

"So, yeah, where *do* you fact-check it?" Deja asked.

"Well," They said. "I check it with my most reliable source—my gut."

"That makes sense. Sometimes your gut makes great calls. You told us to eat our vegetables, and that's good advice." Deja said. "But your gut's not an expert."

"Lots of people believe what I say," They said. "I hear it all the time…. *You know what They say…*"

Gram furrowed her brow. "Constance, just because a lot of people believe what 'They say,' does that make it true?"

Deja continued, "I looked up a lot of these quote unquote 'facts'—some of which I even have heard Mom repeat—and a lot of it was just false! I checked in multiple places! You can't catch a cold by *being* cold, and people use more than 10% of their brains. Also, carrots can't even help you see in the dark.

"If They hasn't done her homework, we don't know if what she says is true. And that means when our friends say, 'You know what They say,' maybe our friends haven't done their homework either. If no one has a source for their information, it's probably best we check it out for ourselves."

The Toy Fox Terrier had stopped skittering about. "Yaaap?" he said sheepishly.

Constance B. Theymselves swayed a little bit back and

forth. Her skin had turned a peculiar shade of orange-green, like it couldn't decide whether she was going to be a little sick or really, really sick.

"Well, children," she said hurrying out the door. "I'm glad you liked my little lesson. Yes, yes. Totally planned. An act of charity, really. And you know what I say: *All's well that ends well!*"

"So They say," said Deja as she crossed her arms and grinned. D'Angelo raised an eyebrow from over on the couch. For the first time, he realized just how funny his kid sister was.

Chapter 3: The Museum of the Misunderstood

Nia liked waking up early. After D'Angelo came along, early mornings were the only time she could get Mom all to herself. Mom was an early riser too. Even though Mom wasn't here, it was a hard habit to break, so she lay in bed, feeling deliciously alone, watching the warm morning light begin to stream through the windows of the Tower.

After a few minutes, Nia got out of bed, took off her sleep bonnet, and walked into the bathroom to start her "program." That was what she called her morning ritual of washing, brushing, and moisturizing. Once done, she went back into the bedroom and gently shook D'Angelo awake.

"D," she whispered.

"Mwhhuzzuhhh," said D.

OK, maybe she was a bit less gentle on the second pass. "Get up, it's morning."

"Murbudubrbur," he replied. Despite his grogginess,

D'Angelo's body was more coordinated than his tongue. He managed to get out of bed and get dressed without opening his eyes.

After leaving Deja behind on their previous trip, Nia had decided to make it up to her by venturing into town again. She was pretty sure she could find a more interesting place than the newspaper office. D'Angelo had been enthusiastic, but to her surprise, Deja had said she wasn't interested.

"I wanna play with the Roof Chickens," she had said. Nia had no idea what this meant and hadn't felt like asking. *Roof Chickens. Fine.* "OK—but no complaining," she had told her sister.

"Roof Chickens," Deja had said again, firmly. "I'll bring tissues."

Nia shrugged. So it was just her and D'Angelo. From the windows in the penthouse, she could see the entire island and all its buildings as if they were dollhouses. She was ready to explore the *places*. But from high up, she couldn't see the people and had sort of forgotten that other people even existed, much less other kids.

But a few minutes and one long elevator ride later, there they were, other kids, sitting with their backs against the Tower: three of them, a girl and two boys. They looked a little older than D'Angelo and a little younger than Nia. Next to them were a couple of skateboards and a battered blue bike. They sat in silence, looking intently at their cell phones.

Nia approached. "Hi! How's it going? We're new here. We're visiting for the summer."

"Hey," said the girl in a monotone voice, without looking up from her screen. She was wearing bright pink sneakers, knee-high rainbow socks, and short overalls. Her hair was a perfectly shaped copper-red afro, and Nia felt sure they would have been friends if they'd met in Brooklyn.

"So…" Nia pushed on, "where's the cool stuff to do in this town?"

"Museum's down there," said the taller of the two boys, pointing behind them without looking up from his phone. He was stick thin with a platinum buzz cut and small square-rimmed glasses that made his blue eyes look huge and a bit wise.

D'Angelo frowned. "What's there to do there?"

The final boy, a heavyset Korean kid dressed in a black shirt, black jeans, and black skate shoes with straight black hair that went down to his chin, sighed theatrically. "Museum stuff."

Nia decided to try again. "I'm Nia and this is D'Angelo. What are your names?"

"Duckle," said the girl.

"Grind_Wizard," said the Korean boy, pronouncing it "Grind Underscore Wizard."

"Bugosaurus," said the boy with glasses.

D'Angelo laughed. "Your parents named you *that*?"

Duckle rolled her eyes. "They're our *screen*names," she said. "We're not going to give you real names, dude. That's PII."

"PII?" asked D'Angelo.

"Personally," said Duckle.

"Identifiable," said Grind_Wizard.

"Information," said Bugosaurus.

D'Angelo snorted. "So? That's the point. We're trying to learn information about you, personally."

Grind_Wizard fixed him with a serious look. "Information is all connected. The more I know about you, the more I can find out. The more I find out, the more I know. Tell me one thing, and eventually, I can know everything."

"That's a little extreme, isn't it?" asked Nia.

Grind_Wizard shrugged. "Suit yourself. But until I know

you IRL, my name is Grind_Wizard."

"But isn't this real life? I'm standing right in front of you!"

Bugosaurus smiled. "Kinda. But Barnaby's Corner is weird. Lots of odd visitors popping in and out. Like you. They come in for a few weeks and act totally different than they do back home. They try on a new personality and new clothes. They meet people and swear they're best friends. It's like they think this whole place is a hologram, and they're holograms too. Then they go home and forget it all."

"So it's real. But it's not *real* real. The *real* real people are like us. They're the same all year round 'cuz Barnaby's Corner isn't just a mirage to them. It's a real place. Those are the ones we can trust."

"And we can't trust you yet," added Duckle.

Nia looked sideways at D'Angelo. This was going nowhere.

"Do you live in the Tower too? We're staying with our grandparents in the penthouse."

"Nah," said Bugosaurus. "We just come here to steal the Wi-Fi. See?" He turned his phone to Nia and D'Angelo, showing a list of Wi-Fi hotspots. The one he was connected to was called "GRAM AND GRAN'S TOTALLY UNSECURED WI-FI."

"Oh…uh….isn't there free Wi-Fi all over this island?"

"Sure." Bugosaurus dropped his voice low. "But if you use that, then *he* knows everything you do on the internet. He can make a profile of you. What you like, what you hate, what your dreams are…"

"He?" Nia asked.

Bugosaurus's voice dropped even further into a husky baritone that seemed strange coming out of a boy who looked a bit like a stick figure. "Barnaby Babel."

D'Angelo perked up at this. "But he disappeared. That's what Phineas Paperplate said."

"*Or did he???*" Grind_Wizard said, his voice dripping with mystery. He echoed his words a few times for effect.

"Mmmm, yeah. That's what Phineas said, so…" Nia interjected.

"*But what if he didn't??*" asked Grind_Wizard, his voice awash with intrigue.

"Anyway," said Nia, "couldn't anyone set up a router and call it TOTALLY UNSECURED WI-FI? What if someone *wants* you to use that Wi-Fi? What if they named it that as a trap?" D'Angelo looked at her with what she thought might almost be admiration.

There was a sudden, deep silence among the three kids. Duckle furrowed her brow. Grind_Wizard looked down at his feet. Bugosaurus closed his huge eyes and winced. They had clearly not considered this possibility.

Just as the silence was becoming truly awkward, Bugosaurus smiled. "I bet you're gonna love the museum." His voice gave no indication of whetherhe meant that as a good thing or a bad thing.

Duckle hopped up, grabbed the bicycle behind her,

and swung her leg over. "Anyway, we're leaving. See you around...if you don't evaporate like the rest of the holograms." The boys grabbed their skateboards, and soon the trio were a block away and disappearing fast.

* * *

Bugosaurus's directions, at least, were straightforward. Nia and D'Angelo found their way to the museum without incident. It did not at all look like the museums they were used to from living in the city. In the city, museums *looked* like museums. When Nia passed one, she knew she was passing a museum. Nia could have passed this place a hundred times and never known it was anything special if it weren't for the sign. It was just a one-story, long, brown building with a saltbox roof in a small grassy lot between two homes. A sign on a purple sandwich board out front said *The Museum of the Misunderstood. OPEN Tuesday 12-6 p.m., Saturday 9-5 p.m., and BY APPOINTMENT.*

It was neither Tuesday nor Saturday, but the lights were on, and the battered red minivan parked out front said PAPERPLATE TAXI SERVICE 555-1212 on it.

D'Angelo yawned for an exaggeratedly long time. "We have total freedom to explore, and you want to go to a museum?"

Nia shrugged. "Well, those kids recommended it to us so..."

"I'm not sure you could call that a recommendation. They didn't seem very excited about it," D'Angelo responded.

"Relax, D," said Nia. "I just want to peek inside. It's

probably air-conditioned, anyhow."

D'Angelo yawned a second time. "You've got five minutes. And if there's a snack bar, you're buying me food."

"Deal."

The museum itself was, in fact, air-conditioned and particularly quiet, perhaps because it was totally empty and dimly lit. "Closed today!" called a voice from the back. D'Angelo shrugged, barely able to hide his smirk, and began to edge toward the door.

"Oh, can we at least look around for a moment?" called Nia. "We're staying with our Gram and Gran, and we have some free time today."

The familiar silhouette of a figure stepped out from a back room and into the light: a wrinkled khaki vest, corduroy jacket, and fedora hat struck quite the outline against the doorframe. Phineas flashed the kids a wide grin. "Kids! Welcome," he said, giving a half-twirl, "to the Museum of the Misunderstood."

"The what?" stammered D'Angelo.

"The Museum of the Misunderstood," he said again as if speaking more slowly would somehow make it all make sense. "You're at our very own museum of surprising and interesting facts— right here in Barnaby's Corner. I'm the chief curator, assistant curator, ticket taker, and intern here. It's a pleasure to have you." Phineas waited for some applause or maybe an ooh or an ahh. None came.

"Hi, Mr. Paperplate. Shouldn't you be at the newspaper

today?" asked Nia.

"Slow news day, kid. Most of them are. So I'm spending the afternoon here in the museum to set up for our next showing. I have several new exhibits to review."

"What do you mean," said D'Angelo. "You don't make these yourself?"

"Oh, heavens no. I told you, I'm just the curator, assistant curator, ticket taker, and intern. I mean, I can't do *everything*! Here in Barnaby's Corner, residents have a tradition of creating the exhibits ourselves. It's local and organic. Come have a look! Here's one sent in by your Gram and Gran."

Phineas walked them both to a mid-sized display window. At the top was a label that read, "A History of Cats," and beneath it, the most curious scene of three cat figurines: There was a paper-mâché figurine of a tuxedo cat with a letter tied around its neck next to a mailbox, a figurine of a calico cat next to a train wearing some type of conductor's hat, and a figurine of a gray striped cat facing what looked to be a bag of firecrackers fixed to its back, pointed toward a large, colorful drawing of a castle.

"What the heck is this?!?" asked D'Angelo.

"It's your grandparents' submission for our next exhibition! We ask people to submit all kinds of strange and wondrous facts to the museum to surprise and delight our patrons. The problem is, a lot of the stuff people send is just—"

"Hot, steaming garbage," said D'Angelo.

"Exactly," Phineas said, appreciating the sentiment, if perhaps not the language. "That's why my job is to review these and display only the good stuff. I'm kind of like a goalie tending the net. I can't let any bad exhibits get past. Any chance you both would help? I can give you free tickets if you do—and of course, ice cream will be on me, all you can eat."

D'Angelo smiled. This was going to be an easy afternoon—free food for a job that looked like it'd take, at most, five minutes. "Sure, Mr. Paperplate. I can already tell you that this one is bull pucky."

"Hang on," said Nia. "You haven't even read the caption!" Two things motivated Nia in a moment like this: her love of cats and her love of playing things by the book. Even though she'd already caught Gram and Gran getting some things wrong—like dressing Deja up in a snowsuit!—she loved the idea of an exhibit on cats and was hoping the caption would clarify whatever misunderstanding D'Angelo had.

"Let's see," she said. "Here we go:"

Cats have played a number of surprising roles throughout history. In the Middle Ages, war manuals suggested tying explosives to the backs of cats from enemy castles, then setting the cats free to run home and set the place ablaze. By the late 1800's, cats were considered for better jobs, with one town in Belgium recruiting cats to deliver its mail. Felines continued to advance in the job world. In the early 2000's, a cat named Tama was made Operating Officer of Kishi Train Station in Japan, eventually overseeing two assistant stationmasters (both cats) and being promoted to Managing Executive Officer of the train company, third in line after the company's president and managing director. – Submitted by Gram and Gran

Nia frowned. That did not sound particularly reliable, and she did not relish hearing D'Angelo tear it down.

"Bull pucky," D'Angelo said again.

"I mean, maybe…?"

"C'mon, Nia. Just, no. I've got a pretty good detector, but this is kinda obvious. Let's get through these displays and get some free ice cream. Hey, Paperplate, we'll do this!"

"Eh?" Phineas had already become distracted attending to another exhibit, but he was more than happy for the help. "Terrific! I have three more for you to look at. Just let me know the thumbs up or thumbs down and then we eat. I'll even throw in fries." Without looking up, Phineas gestured to a hall with three exhibits already set up. D'Angelo and Nia peered into the glass.

The first display was labeled "Discovering America," with the word *discovering* in quotation marks. Inside the case was a globe, a Viking ship, and the Niña, Pinta, and Santa Maria. It was really well put together: polished and smooth and professional-grade. The caption read:

53

"DISCOVERING" AMERICA—Some people say that Christopher Columbus "discovered" America, but of course, there were already many people living here when he arrived. Still, his insight that the Earth is round was revolutionary for his time, and it allowed him to reach the mainland of what we call the U.S. today. Before Columbus, the Vikings, Norse warriors with horns on their helmets, are also said to have made it as far as Canada. – Submitted by Ruthbert R.

"I'm glad this one sets the record straight about Columbus," said Nia. "You can't discover a place where people already live, and he wasn't even the first person here."

"Yeah," said D'Angelo. "This obviously checks out. It's slick and sleek – clearly made by someone who knows what they're doing. What's next?" Nia directed him to the next two exhibits. The first had a courtroom scene that looked pretty standard and was labeled "The Legal System."

"I doubt we even need to read this," said D'Angelo. "Looks fine to m—"

"Hang on," said Nia, as she read the caption:

THE LEGAL SYSTEM—Most countries have some form of legal system that's designed to deliver justice for people. But throughout the Middle Ages, courts also did this for animals, even insects. Pigs, cows, and horses could be convicted of murder, while rats, mice, or slugs might be exiled. For example, after bees stung a person to death, it was reported that the hive was sentenced to suffocation before it could make more honey since people felt the murder bees would be "demonically tainted." This practice is rare, but it has continued. In 2008, for example, a Macedonian bear was convicted of stealing honey, and the government was required to pay thousands of dollars in damages. – Submitted by I.B. Wells

"OK, that's garbage again," said D'Angelo. "The part about charging a bear for stealing honey tipped me off. That's an obvious lie, like something out of *Winnie-the-Pooh*. Looks like this last one is about something futuristic, though," he said, approaching a case that had a model of the Earth and moon in it. "It's titled 'Our Solar System.' Let's see what we have here."

OUR SOLAR SYSTEM—Here on Earth, seasons come from how close the Earth is to the Sun. When we tilt towards it, we have spring and summer. When we tilt away, we have fall and winter. But even though the climate on Earth is warm and hospitable, that isn't true for most of the solar system. The dark side of the moon, for example, is always pitch black, meaning it'd be nearly impossible to set up space stations there. And the moon is cold! You'd need to wear multiple layers, not to mention an oxygen mask, just to move around there. – Submitted by R.B. Rugglesford

Nia was impressed. The display was nicely done, everything shiny and new and looking like it was made by experts. Besides, everything she read sounded familiar, like things she heard in some science class or in a magazine. "OK, D. This is fine, I think."

"Yup," said D'Angelo. "No hits on my bull pucky detector. That's a wrap." He and Nia walked over to Phineas to share what they'd come up with.

"So, did you kids come to any conclusions?" the newspaper editor asked.

"We sure did," said D'Angelo. He shared their findings:

- Discovering America: True
- The Legal System: False
- Our Solar System: True

Two of these look good to us, but one of them is definitely false."

"Oh, dear," said Phineas. "We do get false submissions sometimes. People are always so eager to share what they know that they sometimes pay less attention to whether what they 'know' is worth sharing! Before we grab that ice cream, I just want to confirm: are you both sure?"

D'Angelo nodded, but Nia hesitated. "We need a little more time, Mr. Paperplate. Can you please excuse us?"

She pulled D'Angelo aside, out of earshot of Phineas. "D, are you really sure?"

"Totally. Remember when we tried to figure out who was Gram and who was Gran? All I needed then was to reason things out and follow my gut."

"What does your gut tell you now?"

"That it wants ice cream! And fries!"

But as soon as the words were out, D'Angelo hesitated. Something wasn't right. Going by her "gut" was what Constance B. Theymselves did. Besides, he knew this sort of scenario—the adult lays a careful trap, and then he walks into it and gets a smug "lesson."

Not today.

"Well, I guess it's *possible* this is a trick," D'Angelo said. "There's always some sort of twist, isn't there? So maybe it's something like they're all false—can't be too careful these days. Let's tell Phineas these are all lies."

Do you think D'Angelo is right?
If you were Nia, what would you do to check D'Angelo's gut?
If you'd like a hint, turn the page!

Hint from Phineas

In journalism, we have a saying: "If your mother says she loves you, check it out." Right now, D'Angelo and Nia are relying on their gut instincts. That's well and good, but it will only get them so far, as we learned in the last chapter. In fact, a lot of times, what we think we "know" turns out to be—to borrow a term from D'Angelo—bull pucky. If they really want to know what's what, they'll need to do some searching on their own.

Checking on information to see if it's true is called **independent verification**—you're trying to independently confirm the "facts" someone is sharing against other trusted sources to make sure they're correct. If reliable and totally separate sources say something similar, the information is more likely to be accurate. Online, this is sometimes called **lateral reading**. But whatever you want to call it, the basic idea is that we need to do our homework and actually fact-check the claims people make, *especially* when they seem surprising or outrageous. Big claims require big proof.

In this case, it's D'Angelo and Nia's job to check everything since they need to make sure the museum is credible and trustworthy. However, they haven't done this yet. Can you check the information to determine what should be exhibited and what shouldn't be?

Conclusion: D'Angelo's Bull Pucky Detector Gets a Tune-Up

D'Angelo didn't have much patience for games when ice cream and fries were on the line, so he was pretty annoyed with Phineas's challenge. *Those fries had better be covered in cheese*, he thought. "These are all lies," he pronounced.

"Well," said Phineas. "You're half right. But to know which half, you'd need to look up some of these facts to see which are true and which aren't."

D'Angelo began to protest. Half the stuff here was *definitely* familiar sounding—and the other half was totally crazy. Nia, who'd had her nose in her phone for the past few minutes, looked up.

"Hang on, Mr. P. We want to change our answer. Let's start with "Discovering America." I thought it was true, but it turns out almost the entire thing is incorrect:

- People in 1492 didn't think the Earth was flat.
- Columbus never set foot on mainland North America. He landed in the Caribbean.
- Vikings didn't have horns on their helmets.

So you shouldn't display that one."

D'Angelo's mouth hung agape. He was certain he'd heard all these things in school, if not from his teachers, then from his friends or an online video. His diorama in 6th grade definitely had horns on Viking helmets, and his teacher hadn't said anything. He'd gotten a B+. Besides, this display had looked so polished – how could something that looked so nice be wrong?

"C'mon, Nia. Next thing you'll tell me that his ships weren't called the *Niña*, *Pinta*, and *Santa Maria*."

"They weren't! Technically, they were named *la Santa Clara, la Pinta*, and *la Santa Gallega*."

"Show off." *This is troubling information*, thought D'Angelo, *but I guess it isn't totally surprising*. People got things wrong all the time, and few folks bothered to double-check what they said. As a rule, D'Angelo didn't trust anyone unless he had good reason to.

"OK, so I was right. *All* of these are lies."

Phineas smiled. "Well, you'd be correct about the space exhibit. Even though people talk about the 'dark side' of the moon, there isn't one. The moon's rotation is synchronized with Earth's, so there is always a part facing away from us. But it isn't always dark. In fact, all parts of the moon get light—*and* they get really hot—like 250 degrees Fahrenheit hot…enough to boil water!"

"What about the seasons?" asked Nia. "I definitely remember something about that from somewhere."

"It's a common misconception. The reason we have seasons is because sometimes we are tilted into the sun's direct rays, and sometimes we get them on an angle. But it's *not* about how close we are."

"No way," said D'Angelo. "This was just too professional-looking. It's clearly real."

Phineas shrugged. "That might have worked when your mom and I were kids, but these days robots and artificial intelligence can make anything look slick. Why, with the touch of a few buttons, you can conjure up any photographic evidence you want." He pulled a small scrap of paper out of his wallet. "Did you know I won the Olympic gold for poodle clipping?" He held up an old, black-and-white photo of himself standing next to a poodle and holding a large gold medal.

"Wow, no!" said Nia.

"That's because it never happened," he said. "The event is just an urban legend—an April Fools' Day prank."

"Wait, so why would you even have that?" asked D'Angelo.

"Well, it seemed like something I might need one day. And I just did! My point is, *looking* true isn't the same as *being* true."

D'Angelo was livid. He did not like looking foolish—especially in front of Nia—and he really wanted his food now. Best to just give the adult what he wanted. "Fine. We're really sorry, Mr. P. We got tricked the way most people do. Let's discuss it over ice cream. At least we nixed the exhibit on the legal system."

Nia interrupted. "Actually, D, that one's true! I looked it up. People debate how *much* of this happened, but it definitely occurred. Animals really were put on trial. And that story about the bear in Macedonia definitely happened. Maybe your 'bull pucky detector' needs some tuning." She was playing like she was trying to be helpful, but D'Angelo knew his sister was enjoying every second of this. Like the time he said the capital of Iowa was "Dez Moynes" and Nia announced, "Actually, it's pronounced *De Moyn*." She'd found a way to work it into conversation at least five times after that.

If there was one thing D'Angelo didn't enjoy, it was anyone showing him up—especially his sister. So if she and Phineas wanted to play the "looking things up" game, he could do that too. After a few minutes stewing in his own frustration, he whipped around.

"Aha!" he said, waving his phone in Nia's face. "You both think you're so clever, but you missed one thing. We all agreed that the exhibit on cats was incorrect, but I just looked it up, and every single fact checks out. Cats with fire-crackers. Cats running train stations. Cats delivering mail. True, true, and true. Gram and Gran aren't wrong, they're just weird. I found the information from multiple sources."

Phineas smiled from ear to ear. "There you go, my boy! That's the spirit. Just because something sounds true—or false—doesn't mean it's so. That's why we have to check. I feel like that insight deserves some ice cream, don't you?"

Nia jutted in. "And tickets!"

"And tickets. But since you both got fooled, I'll ask

you to do the job of letting anyone who submitted incorrect exhibits know. Looks like both of them came from the same person, too." Phineas scribbled something down on a scrap of paper and handed it to Nia.

It read: *Ruthbert Rugglesford, #1 Underbridge Terrace.*

"At your earliest convenience, pop by his house and explain why we can't use his exhibits. Unless, of course, you want to experiment with having a cat deliver the note," Phineas said with a chuckle.

D'Angelo was unamused, but hungry as he was, he didn't protest. Besides, it'd be another reason to get out of the Tower and explore a bit more. Whoever Ruthbert Rugglesford was, D'Angelo was looking forward to correcting him and setting the record straight. More than that, though, he was looking forward to free food.

Chapter 4: The Reviews Are In

Nia and D'Angelo had intended to see this Mr. Rugglesford immediately, but things kept getting in the way. Gram and Gran's hobbies were one example.

During the first few weeks they stayed with their grandparents, Nia, D'Angelo, and Deja got to learn all about their hobbies, most of which were decidedly odd. (Gram called them "side hustles," but as best the kids could tell, none of them actually made money.)

Gran spent many of his afternoons building dollhouses that could be placed inside other dollhouses. ("So the dolls will have something to play with!")

Gram, meanwhile, was teaching the rooftop chickens to do a dance called the *Tarantella*—which was even harder to do than it was to pronounce. ("Aren't you afraid the chickens will fall off the roof?" Nia had asked. "Well, chickens are birds, and They say all birds can fly," Gram had replied.)

But Gram and Gran's favorite "hobby" was something so ordinary it didn't feel much like a hobby at all.

"Brunch!" they'd both shout and clap their hands with glee around 11 a.m. each day. And, each day, the five of them would ride the elevator down all seventy-seven floors of the great, green Tower and amble about Barnaby's Corner in search of something to nosh on.

"Are you sure eating counts as a hobby, Gram?" Deja had asked on one of their first trips.

"Only if you do it well," Gram winked.

Gram said she hadn't always been an adventurous eater, but after discovering online reviews, she now made a point of ordering the weirdest thing on the menu wherever they went: anchovy buttercup bagels, smoked asparagus milkshakes, pickled turnip in cackleberry compote, truffled salamander eggs with maple-clotted cream and truffle aioli. She figured if other people could try it, so could she.

"If it sounds like trouble, make mine a double!" hooted Gram with glee as she'd hunt through a menu for something unique and surprising.

Gran was nearly the opposite. Once he found something at a restaurant he liked, it was the only thing he'd order. "Why tempt fate?" he'd say. "I already know what I like, and the whole reason I came is to eat something I like!" Gram had pointed out that this usually meant something deep-fried, and Gran happily agreed. This was an early point of connection for him and D'Angelo, who also liked any food that ended in the letters "-ers"—smackers, slammers, sliders, crispers, chompers—they loved 'em all. Deja did, too, though she would basically try anything one of her siblings recommended.

On this particular morning there was a slight breeze, and Nia noticed Gram had brought along a silk scarf with a print of Paris and the Eiffel Tower on it. Paris was the City of Lights: the inspiration of James Baldwin, Josephine Baker, and Quincy Jones. Mom had schooled her in the city's importance, but that wasn't why she was thinking of Paris. Now that Nia was entering high school, she'd be able to join the French Club. She'd heard from her neighbor Stacey Stoneback—who was already a sophomore and well versed in school comings and goings—that every other year the club raised money to travel to Paris themselves.

"Those people are *all* my best friends now," Stacey had said with a far-off look after joining last year's trip. Nia had thought that sounded nice, though she'd never actually seen the other students hang out with Stacey.

"Gram, have you ever been to Paris?" Nia asked as they made their way across town.

"Well, of course!" said Gram cheerfully. "Long time ago. Gran and I stayed with friends in this colossal house—it had tons of mirrors, a whole hallway full of them!" Gram spread her arms to underscore her point. "Odd people, our friends. At every meal, they told Gran and me that the only thing they had to eat was cake—heaps and heaps of it! At the time, an all-cake diet sounded positively revolutionary."

Gram sighed. "But it turns out they made one crucial mistake. They had plenty of cake but not a drop of frosting in sight. And no milk to wash it down! That's when Gran and I decided to skedaddle. Come to think of it, Nia, I was thinking we might try the new French restaurant at the other end of town. Any interest?"

Nia's ears perked. She'd never had French food before, and this could be her in with the club. From what she'd read, the portions were a bit smaller because the food was rather filling: creamy and rich and full of butter. It sounded perfect.

* * *

A small red-and-white striped awning jutted out at the end of the block. Beneath its wing stood a short but smartly dressed man with thinning black hair and shoes that shined like over-polished chrome in the midday sun. Above it read: "Monterey Jack's Totally Authentic 100% Real and Certainly Not Bogus Italian Restaurant and Cheese-arium." It was a rather large sign.

"Good morning, Monty!" Gran shouted to Mr. Jack, the owner of the restaurant. He had to speak up since the determined thumping of a bass echoed from whatever music was playing inside.

"Buongiorno, Gran! Fine day it is—just took some extra crispy bacon-jalapeno-cheddar-gorgonzola poppers out of the oven. Nice and spicy, just like we do in *Italia*." He pronounced the last word "Eeeetalia." It felt to Nia like he'd practiced the pronunciation more than once.

D'Angelo, who until that moment had been preoccupied with some video, perked up and asked if he could use the bathroom. This seemed like the kind of place that would have a nice one.

"Of course! And who, may I ask, are these young companions?" Mr. Jack said with a small bow.

"We're his grandchildren!" piped in Deja, always happy for some attention, especially any from someone in a position to give her food.

"Oh-ho!" said Mr. Jack. "I guess it never occurred to me you actually *were* grandparents!"

"Funny thing," said Gram. "For a long time, it didn't occur to us either! We've been called Gram and Gran as far back as we can remember. Made for some awkward moments in grade school…"

As the adults chatted, D'Angelo stood mouth agape at the interior of Monterey Jack's Totally Authentic 100% Real and Certainly Not Bogus Italian Restaurant and Cheese-arium, which was a bit like going to an arcade with the volume turned up. He'd reached the bathroom, but now a challenge presented itself.

One door said "Spaghetti," and the other read "Linguini." But which to choose?

D'Angelo knew this had to be a quality restaurant, one whose patrons would know which type of pasta meant "this room has a urinal" and which did not. If they'd taught this thing in school, he'd certainly have paid more attention. As it was, he closed his eyes (hoping it would make him invisible) and ran into the door on the left, "Spaghetti."

As it turned out, "Spaghetti" was the correct choice. The bathroom was clean and decorated in a white subway tile, with helpful signs reminding the people who worked there to wash their hands. (D'Angelo saw this in so many restaurants; adults could be so forgetful!) The bathroom even had high-quality graffiti, like a website address labeled "The TRUTH About the Pyramids." D'Angelo wrote that down to check out later. He always did think those pyramids were a little too obvious not to be a conspiracy. "That settles it," he thought. "This place is definitely high class."

Back outside, D'Angelo rushed over to his sisters. "Deja, Nia, we *have* to go here. I've gotta try their pizza."

"What do you mean, D? We live in *Brooklyn*. Every store has pizza, even the ones that aren't restaurants."

"Nah. This place is the real deal. It's a *cheese-arium*."

"Yay!" said Deja, completely sold.

"I do love me a good popper," nodded Gran, having eavesdropped on the whole conversation.

But Gram crinkled her nose and glanced at Gran from the corner of her eye. "Actually, Nia and I were thinking we'd try the new French cafe today," she said without turning her head. "Let's have poppers another time, Monty."

"But poppers are plenty adventurous, Gram!" Gran pleaded. "Sometimes I think you won't eat anything that looks like food. You know children, one time Gram took me to a restaurant, and she ended up drinking grass juice out of an open-toed cowboy boot. Who ever heard of such a thing?"

"What's grass juice?" asked Deja.

"Nobody knows!" cried Gran.

"Oh, Gran, you know full well it's juice that's squeezed from grass clippings," said Gram tolerantly. "No mystery about it. It's just like it says."

"What's it taste like?" asked Nia.

"Well, the leathery flavor of the boot was pretty strong, but I'd say mostly it tasted like grass. And a little like chicken," Gram shrugged. "But adventurous or not, poppers aren't French, and I've got my mind set on that cafe." Nia shrugged her shoulders at D'Angelo, relieved that Gram had intervened.

"Suit yourself!" Monterey Jack turned his attention back to a set of outdoor tables he was preparing for the lunchtime rush, and the group walked on. The thumping bass sound followed them for the rest of the block. A few shops past that, they paused at the most delightful scent, something like a mix of butterscotch and warm hugs.

"Heya, Bea," said Gram with a wave.

Beatrix Ramekin owned The Chocolate Chippery, one of Barnaby Corner's oldest establishments and a staple of the downtown. In the window were all sorts of baking tools and sassy signs written in colorful chalk, things like: "I eat a balanced diet: one cookie in each hand," and "I'm really into fitness—fitness entire cookie in my mouth!"

"Gooday Gram, Gooday Gran," said Ms. B as she pushed forward a tray of samples. "Care to sample my new extra crispy CHOCOLATE-bacon-jalapeno-cheddar-gorgonzola poppers? Don't be fooled by the name. They're made entirely of chocolate. It's just marketing, you know. Give the people what they want." Before she could finish, D'Angelo had stuffed one in his mouth and was handing another to Deja.

"Glamphoo ferrymush," said Deja with the only part of her mouth that wasn't already occupied, devouring what appeared to be a slightly melted hunk of chocolate decorated with frosting, sugar, and rainbow sprinkles.

"Glad you like these, children! Come back when you're ready for more. First popper is free, but the second costs double!" Ms. Ramekin spread her hands across her gingham apron as though she were wiping off flour or sugar, but in fact, her hands—and her entire outfit—were spotless.

Two blocks down, the group paused again in front of Cha-Cha's Salsaria. This time, the kids saw a familiar face. Phineas Paperplate was deep in conversation with the manager, Luis Muñoz. "Oh, hey kids! We're just planning for the Babel Festival, honoring our town's founder."

"That's the guy who vanished, right?" said D'Angelo, still curious about the fate of Barnaby Babel and sensing that it was the best mystery this small town had to offer.

"That's right," said Paperplate. "He vanished thirty years ago this summer. The paper's doing a big retrospective on it. And Mr. Muñoz has promised his restaurant will cook their famous extra crispy *salsa-infused*-bacon-jalapeno-cheddar-gorgonzola poppers! They're a crowd favorite."

While D'Angelo tried to pump Phineas for details (about Babel AND the poppers), Nia's mind started to wander. The mere mention of cooking was enough for her to grab her stomach, which had been sounding a dull roar for the past twenty minutes.

"Hey, Gram, are we about ready to eat?" she asked. A short bit later, the group turned the corner, and the French restaurant came into view.

Le Petit Café shimmered a bit like a desert mirage. Canopied by cerulean blue umbrellas, its storefront was surrounded by flowers of various colors and sizes. Large fans, with blades shaped like palm leaves, created a cool breeze that rustled the tables just enough to make them appear alive. Soft music piped in from an unseen speaker:

Essayez les trucs gris, c'est délicieux.

Vous ne me croyez pas? Demandez les plats.

Nia had no idea what that meant, but everything about it just seemed magical—both very, very old and very, very new all at once. Even before taking a bite, she was in love.

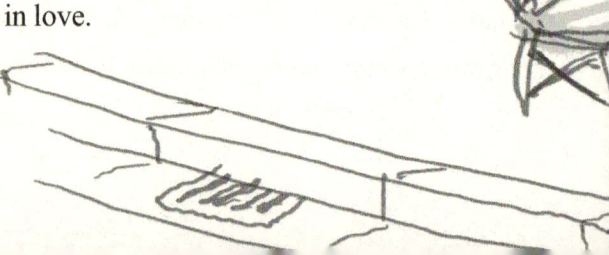

And then it happened.

"Hang on, crew. I think we need to hold off on this," came Gran's voice from the back of their group.

"I've just read some of the comments for this place on NoshMonster, a site that collects user reviews," he said, waving his phone as he spoke. "It looks like a no-go to me. They're all terrible! It has an average rating of 1.3 out of five stars."

Nia's heart sank. Gran and Gram had been using NoshMonster for years to find the best places to eat, and they trusted it implicitly.

"Looks like it's poppers time," Gran shrugged, bouncing back quickly. "Shall we, D'Angelo?"

But D'Angelo didn't hear him. He was studying his sister's expression. "What's the matter with you?" he asked. In a huff that she hoped didn't sound too much like a sob, Nia explained her Paris dream, her hope that she'd get to try French food, her goal of joining French club, and her extreme hunger. And without her saying it, and though he'd never admit to it, D'Angelo knew what Nia was really hoping for: a way to make high school a little less scary next year.

"I guess I won't get to try this food today. I was…never mind," Nia said, her shoulders dropping a full two inches.

D'Angelo thought for a moment, glancing at his sister, then at Gram and Gran, then at Le Petit Café. "Gram, would you and Gran mind sharing the reviews for Le Petit Café with us?"

"Sure thing, sweetie. This one seems pretty open-and-shut, though," said Gram, who by now had looked up the restaurant herself. "There are only three reviews, but they are pretty consistent. Take a look,"

"Meh." - 1/5 stars
Why on Earth would you spend your time at Le Petit Café when there are perfectly great options all throughout Barnaby's Corner? I came by to sample their desserts, and they were completely unimpressive. Tarts? Eclairs? Crème Brûlée? Give me an old-fashioned cookie any day over this fancy 'French' cuisine. Yeah, no. - BR

"Rude Staff - Not Worth Your Time" - 2/5 stars
Le Petit Café, like many French restaurants, has terrible service. I made a reservation for 2 p.m. last week, and when I arrived that evening, I asked for an outdoor table so I could watch the sunset. Not only would they not let me eat outside, but they said they didn't even have a table for me because they were "booked." I wound up getting into a huge fight with my friend while there

— she said I have a bubble butt! — and the afternoon was just ruined. (I have since consulted many doctors, and they have assured me that my butt isn't the slightest bit bubbly.) Better to spend your time at a place that knows how to treat its customers right. - MJ

"Bland" - 1/5 stars
Food is meant to have spice. That's what makes it joyful. But the food at Le Petit Café is so creamy and rich, nothing like what you'd expect from a great meal. And not a single popper. How am I supposed to eat like this? Fortunately, there are better options right around the corner. - L. M.

Gram frowned as she read off the reviews. "Well, I was really hoping we'd have a winner in this new restaurant, but I guess that's not in the cards. No matter, plenty of other options."

Nia piped in, having done some research of her own. "Hang on. Look at this! The newspaper reviewed Le Petit Café last week, and they liked them just fine."

Le Petit Café – 4.5/5 stars
This charming new bistro is a welcome addition to

Barnaby's Corner. Chef Pierre Gruyere cooks up a variety of French classics, including a delicious saucisson sandwich, light and airy croissants, and a custard tart that is as good as if it came from the streets of Paris. The interior is clean but a bit cramped, so grab the outdoor seating for a relaxing experience. – Phineas Paperplate

"See?" said Nia. "The newspaper says the cafe is worth trying."

"It does," said Gram hesitantly. "But the score is still three reviews to one. I trust Phineas, but the masses have spoken."

Nia and the group turned to head back from where they came, but as they began to leave, a smirk stretched across D'Angelo's face. He'd worked something out in his head, and he was rather proud of himself.

"Hold up. I can't guarantee we'll like French food, but I can tell you this restaurant isn't nearly as bad as the online reviews say. In fact, I think we should definitely give it a try."

"D, you can't possibly know that," said Nia, who was doing her best to hide how sulky she felt.

"Actually, sis, I can."

D'Angelo is confident he should ignore the negative reviews of Le Petit Café. Are you?
Turn the page for a hint.

Hint from D'Angelo

I sometimes use reviews to help me decide if something is worth my time, but not all reviews are created equal. Everyone has their own perspective. That's not a bad thing, but it means everyone views the world with some amount of **bias**. For example, a soccer player may visit her local park and decide it's great because the fields are flat and large, while a basketball player might conclude the same park is terrible because the basketball hoops need repairs. It's the same park, but how people describe things depends on their perspective.

Bias is natural. Everyone has it, even you and me! It's hard to know everyone's biases, and many people don't even realize they have them. But that's why we need to **consider the source** whenever we read information. What's their perspective? Do they have a **clear reason to be biased**?

Think about where we get our information and whether the people sharing that information may be likely to skew it in a certain way, either by accident or because it benefits them. Can you detect a possible bias in any of the sources here? Re-read the chapter carefully!

Conclusion: Today's Special—Deep-Fried Bias

D'Angelo turned to Nia. "Personally, the main thing I trust is my own tastebuds, but can you tell Gram why you trust the newspaper?"

Nia smiled weakly. "We know the newspaper here is probably trustworthy. Mom told us that, and so did Gram and Gran. The Barnaby Star has earned their trust over the years. So, I know I can rely on their review to be as fair as possible. The review pointed out both positives (the food) and negatives (the cramped indoor space), and it feels like it tried to give us an unbiased view."

"Thanks!"

Nia turned around with a start. Phineas Paperplate was standing right behind her.

"No need to stop on my account," he said, tipping his hat.

Nia was nervous. Even if the newspaper review could be trusted, she already knew that wouldn't be enough to convince Gram to try the place. Until a few years ago, Gram ate peanut butter sandwiches, cold cereal, and cake exclusively, and she only started trying new foods once she could see how many other people were doing it on NoshMonster. The site had really done her good—maybe even *too much good*, considering her newfound love for grass juice served from an open-toed boot.

Nia knew more would be needed to sway Gram. "That's

fine, D. But how do you know the other reviews are bad?"

"Good question, sis. The official term for them, I believe, is bull pucky. Because you can't trust a single word. Gram, who were the authors of the three reviews?"

Gram read out the list: BR, MJ, and L.M.—also known as Beatrix Ramekin, Monterey Jack, and Luis Muñoz—all the owners or managers of competing downtown restaurants.

"Oh-ho!" said Gran. "This means they all have a likely bias. They'll stand to lose money if everyone starts going to this new restaurant, so they have a strong incentive to bad-mouth it. They aren't fair observers!"

"Exactly," said D'Angelo with a confident grin. "Wouldn't you agree, Mr. Paperplate?"

Phineas smiled and hooked his fingers onto his corduroy vest. Deja thought he must be mighty hot wearing a vest and jacket in the summer, but mostly she thought it would be great if everyone could resolve this debate so she could get some food.

"Indeed," Phineas said. "In fact, all three of those reviews on NoshMonster wouldn't have made it into my newspaper even if they *had* been written by an unbiased source. Those reviewers played the ol' switcheroo. They said they were reviewing the restaurant, but they talked about other things. For example, it's not the restaurant's fault for being full if one reviewer showed up hours late for their reservation. Monterey Jack said he had a 2 p.m. seating but arrived in time for the sunset! I do feel bad about the bubble butt affair, but it's unfair to criticize a restaurant for the behavior of a customer. Lots of online reviews do this sort of thing. They're more about the reviewer than they are about what's being reviewed."

"I get it," said D'Angelo. "So when Mr. Muñoz criticizes the French food for not having spice, he's not being fair because French food isn't *supposed* to be spicy."

The group now began walking toward Le Petit Café. "That's right," said Phineas with a wink. "If I hired Deja to review a hip hop album, but she said it stunk because she hates hip hop, she's not being a fair reviewer. Her job is to tell me if it's good or bad hip hop, so she has to keep an open mind and try to stay fair. These reviews are anything but that."

Phineas joined the family for what turned out to be the best brunch they'd had so far. Nia did, in fact, wind up loving French food, so much so that she barely spoke or looked up from her plate. She did, however, manage to flash D'Angelo an exhausted, appreciative smile.

D'Angelo nodded. He wasn't personally a fan of French food—there not being any poppers on the menu—but he did have to admit that being right tasted rather sweet.

Chapter 5: Gran's Special Medicine

"What. Is. That. Smell?" asked Nia as she jumped out of bed and undid her hair wrap. During the early hours, an odor had crept its way down the hall and across the threshold of the kids' room. It smelled like forty eggs had gone rotten, been left out in the sun, and then been abducted by a madman skunk. If Gram and Gran had wallpaper, it most definitely would have peeled itself off the wall.

D'Angelo had built himself a makeshift gas mask from his t-shirt while Deja hid under the covers, softly sobbing, her face buried in the mattress.

"Oh?" said Gram, who happened to be walking by at the moment. "That's just Gran."

Nia's eyes were beginning to water a bit. "Care to elaborate, Gram?"

"Sure! Gran takes pills once a week to help him grow taller, but as a side effect, he becomes quite flatulent."

"Flatulent?" asked Deja, momentarily distracted by a new word. Vocabulary had been her strongest subject last year, and she was determined to keep her streak going.

"It means gassy," said her sister.

"Oh."

"Well, usually I'd just wait it out, but my friends Ms. Maplethorp and Ms. Thistlebottom are coming to visit today, so I'll need to keep him hidden away in the room with you," Gram said.

D'Angelo sprang up and would have said something he'd later have regretted, but Nia spoke quickly to cut him off.

"Gram, why does Gran want to be taller?"

"You know, dear, when one gets older, one starts to shrink. And as Gran and I are quite old, we've been shrinking for quite a while now. We both used to be much taller." Her eyes sparkled like faraway stars. "Yes, your Gran used to cut a towering figure. Used to heckle our friend Napoleon about it all the time. He disliked Gran on account of getting a crick in his neck from always looking up to him."

"Gram...how old are you and Gran anyway?"

"I suppose we lost track. But one thing's for sure: I'm just a little bit older than he is. And you can count on that."

* * *

Most smells become less noticeable with time, but somehow the longer it went on, the worse the funk became. And now the smells were joined by sounds: deep, rumbling sounds;

high, whining sounds. Imagine tying a big balloon to the back of a motorcycle and then letting the air out of it while you drive the motorcycle around. That's what it sounded like.

Deja looked horrified. "Are those sounds also *flatulence*?" she asked. In spite of their dire situation, she could not help being proud of herself for learning a new word.

"Yes indeed," replied Gram. "I guess I don't mind them too much. Kinda reminds me of the time we tied a big balloon to the back of a motorcycle and drove it around. Those were the days."

As much as she wanted to know *why* anyone would tie a big balloon to the back of a motorcycle, Nia decided she had to take action.

"Gram, would you mind giving us a moment to get dressed? We'll be out shortly."

"Of course, child! I'll close the door on my way out." Gram smiled pleasantly at her. "Not that it'll do much good about the sound…or the smell. Sorry, lovely dove, but that's medicine for you. Side-effects."

As soon as the door closed, D'Angelo started talking. His voice was muffled by the shirt he was holding over his face, but his panic was perfectly clear. "I *told* you coming here was a mistake. I *told* you Gram and Gran were up to something. Well, here's Exhibit A, and it's right under your nose, Nia."

Tears began to stream down Deja's face. Nia couldn't tell whether she was crying or her eyes were just watering from the odor.

"It's too loud! I can't hear myself think!" Deja wailed. Her words were punctuated by an absolutely ghastly noise from the other room. It started like a bullfrog stuck in a metal pipe and then swelled and swelled, rumbling until the windows of their room began to rattle before ending suddenly with a buzz like an angry fly getting sucked into a vacuum cleaner.

"Maybe we can convince him to stop taking those pills," suggested Nia.

D'Angelo shook his head. "Oh no. No way. *I'm* not going anywhere. I'm barely keeping my cookies in as it is!"

"But—" Nia started.

"Don't make me do it," sobbed Deja. "I...I just can't."

She has a way of making herself look utterly helpless that is just plain unfair, Nia thought. Then again, she still felt a little guilty for having abandoned Deja the day after they arrived. Here was a chance to make things even.

"OK," she said. "You two stay here. I'll handle this."

* * *

Gran sat at the table with the most curious array of pills before him: green ones, yellow ones, pills that were polka dot pink. Three of them were shaped like triangles and two like little stars. One was so large it looked like a slice of orange-marmalade cake, which in retrospect, perhaps it was. A few were so small they looked like tiny pearls. Were the smell not so bad, Nia would have taken more time to explore.

"Gran, why are you taking so many pills?"

"Oh, hi there, Nia! These are to help me grow taller, of course. I used to be such a tall man. People used to look up to me. I played center on our high school basketball team. They even had a nickname for me."

"Really? What was it?"

"They called me…" Gran opened his arms wide and wiggled his eyebrows, "*The Tall Man*."

"Oh."

"Because I was a tall man, you see. But I've been shrinking for what feels like thousands of years. Nobody calls me that anymore. I used to be able to look a giraffe right in the eye. Do you know what that's like? It's wonderful. Majestic. Nowadays, I wouldn't be able to do it without using a hot-air balloon."

"I don't think giraffes are *that* tall, Gran."

Gran shrugged. "I remember 'em being miles and miles tall. Maybe they've all shrunk with age too."

"Gran, I don't think you can grow much taller at your age, and these pills are making you…um…they're creating an unpleasant situation."

Gran paused from sorting pills and looked up. "Sorry about that, kiddo. But these are from my doctor, so I'm pretty sure they're fine."

"Wait, your *doctor* prescribed these?"

"Not my *doctor* doctor, my *online* doctor, Dr. Asmodeus

P. Hornswoggle."

"That doesn't sound like a real name, Gran," Nia said. "Besides, can't anyone just put the word 'Doctor' in front of their name online?"

Gran paused. He hadn't considered that before. "I don't know. I'm pretty sure he's a real doctor. He keeps saying 'I'm a real doctor.' I don't think he'd say that if he weren't. But tell ya what, let's fire up the ol' computer and take a look at his website. That way I can put your mind at ease."

It's not my mind I'm worried about, it's my nose, thought Nia.

Gran stood up boldly. "To the Computer Room!" he cried.

"The Computer Room? But don't you have a laptop right here?" asked Nia.

"That thing? That's just a toy. If we're going to do this, let's do it right!"

* * *

To Nia's surprise, Gran led her into the elevator.

"I wonder if you've noticed something special about this elevator," he said.

Nia looked around. It looked like a normal, if very fancy, elevator, with wood paneling, chrome accents, and soft light glowing from tastefully recessed light fixtures. She studied the elevator panel. It looked pretty ordinary too. Door open and close buttons. A call button and an emergency button. A bunch of buttons with numbers on them. Except…

"Why is there a zero?" she asked.

"Good eye! I'm impressed."

"Is there a zero-eth floor?" she said, hoping that there might be. She remembered how thrilling, and just a little bit scary, it had been in *Charlie and the Great Glass Elevator* when Charlie Bucket had taken the elevator into Minus Land.

Gran shook his head sadly. "That would be wonderful, wouldn't it? But no, there's no zero-eth floor. If you press it by itself, it doesn't do anything at all. BUT if you would press the buttons in the following order…"

Nia hovered her hand over the panel, ready to follow Gran's instructions.

"Zero. Zero. One. One. One. One. One. One."

A faint, pleasant ding sounded, and the doors slid shut.

"Two zeroes, six ones. Remember that," Gran said.

Nia had a sudden moment of panic when she realized that she was now trapped in the elevator with an old man experiencing medically enhanced farts. But to her relief, the elevator didn't go more than two or three floors before it stopped, and the doors opened up.

Whatever Nia was expecting, it wasn't this. In front of her was a gigantic room, capped by ceilings thirty feet high. It must have been as wide as an entire floor of the Tower, and as deep, too. Against each of the walls, there were floor-to-ceiling cases made of green-tinted glass filled with electronics. And in the center of the room, in neat rows and columns, were clear glass cases, each eight feet long, six feet wide, and fifteen feet tall. The tops of the cases were covered with a dense network of cords, wires, and pipes carrying luminous blue and purple liquids into the upper reaches of the room so that in some places, it was impossible to see the ceiling, and in others, Nia could see all the way up.

Nia suddenly understood. "The computer room isn't a room with a computer in it," she said to Gran. "The room *is* the computer."

Gran chuckled. "Yup. Here, let me show you to the user interface." He started down one of the rows of cases with Nia walking briskly to stay by his side, instead of directly behind him, in the "danger zone." As they walked, she investigated the cases they were passing and saw the following:

- A case entirely filled with a thick, green gas which emitted bursts of red and blue light from its interior.
- An old, wooden desk with a large, leather-bound encyclopedia volume (MARMALADE-NEMATODE) open on it. Above the desk, a giant electronic eyeball on a mechanical arm was slowly and carefully reading. As Nia walked by, it turned to look at her with interest.
- A mouse-wheel with a serious, intense, little white mouse running inside it. Gran stopped here briefly and said, "Benji, Nia. Nia, Benji. Benji is my computer mouse." Benji did not stop running, but Nia could swear he turned his head and nodded. She waved at him and smiled.
- Drawers full of white cards with square holes punched

in them in different patterns.
- A ladder bolted to the wall leading up to a hatch in the ceiling. ("That's the emergency ladder," Gran explained. "That hatch goes up into our bedroom closet. We could've used it to get down here, but the elevator is fancier and takes much less time.")

"All this stuff is part of the computer?" Nia asked, her eyes wide.

"That's why it's here," said Gran, as his stomach made a deep, ominous rumble.

"Do you know how all of it works?"

"Of course I do. I'm a world-class computer expert," responded Gran with pride. "I practically invented the internet."

"Can you show me how it works?"

"Sorry, kiddo. I haven't invented a way to explain it to anyone else yet."

They turned a corner, and Nia saw their destination. Against the wall, there was a battered old computer desk with a fifteen-inch monitor on it and a dull gray keyboard. Next to the monitor was an ancient-looking printer, and in front of the desk was a comically small, forest-green computer chair bearing several dark stains. Its seat was so worn down that she could see the internal foam in places. Littered around the desk were half-opened reams of paper, empty ballpoint pens, broken pencils, post-its with vague scribbles on them, a few coffee mugs, and an empty Styrofoam container, which Nia guessed used to be full of Chinese takeout. Surrounding all of it was a wall of cardboard boxes that formed the rough outline of a small room in which the desk sat. The boxes were covered with white labels bearing the following black letters: "**FLOPPIES. ISTANBUL VACATION PIX? DOCUMENTATION. MISCELLANEOUS. EMERGENCY ONLY. RECEIPTS. GRAM 1892-1925. ARPANET CORRESPONDENCE,**" and the tantalizing "**DO NOT OPEN THIS MEANS YOU.**"

Gran gestured grandly. "The user interface!" he declared. "What do you think?"

"It's…uh…I don't know. I guess I expected something more hi-tech?"

"It's a little grubby, I guess," shrugged Gran, "but it's what's under the hood that counts. Let's fire it up and check out Dr. Hornswoggle's website so I can put your mind at ease. You'll be so proud when you have a big, tall Grandpa instead of a small bean of a Gran. Isn't that what you kids call tiny things? Small beans?"

Gran pressed a power button on the keyboard. In a few moments, he brought up the website on the monitor.

It was well put together, with muted colors and various tabs at the top that offered more information: ABOUT ME, INFORMATION, CONTACT US, TESTIMONIALS, and COMMUNITY. In the center of the page were two photographs. One picture was of an open bottle of the pills Nia had seen Gran taking. The other was a picture of a smiling man wearing a lab coat. He appeared about fifty years old with a deep bronze tan and gleaming white teeth. Underneath, a caption identified him as DR. ASMODEUS P. HORNSWOGGLE.

"Welcome to my website," Nia read. "I am Dr. Asmodeus P. Hornswoggle, a real doctor, and for twenty years, I have been giving the height-challenged hope that they can live a taller life. Many people think that what I offer is impossible. As a real doctor, I understand their worries. I invite you to experience this website, learn about Verticol, and decide for yourself whether it's right for you."

"I am confident that you will decide to take the Verticol plunge! Verticol is a proprietary blend of vitamins and rare earth minerals specially formulated to lengthen the human body."

Nia stopped. "What does *proprietary* mean, Gran?

"It means that Dr. Hornswoggle owns the recipe for Verticol. It's his property and he has to keep it a secret so nobody else can steal it. That's how you know it's good. Everyone wants to steal it!"

"But then how do we really know what's in it?"

"I guess we don't, but your Gram won't tell me what's in her famous rosemary-pecan-rhubarb cobbler either, and I gobble that stuff up." Gran smacked his lips.

Nia returned to reading. "In fact, a recent study being conducted by my very own MacGuffin Institute shows promising early results that Verticol might help test subjects gain 2.5 inches in height. You can't make this up! So please

Dr. Asmodeus P. Hornswoggle, MD
(real doctor)

About Me **Information** **Contact Us**

Testimonials **Community**

Asmodeus P. Hornswoggle

Welcome to my website,

I am Asmodeus P. Hornswoggle, a real doctor, and for twenty years, I have been giving the

make yourself at home. Read about the research into Verticol. Discover how it works. Or just visit our online community of Vertifans and say 'high.' (That's just a little joke we have.)"

"Huh. I like that he's telling you to make up your own mind," Nia said.

"See? He's on the up-and-up."

Nia thought for a moment. "A testimonial is like a review, right? Maybe we should check those out."

"It's even better than a review," said Gran. "A review can be from any old person, but a *testimonial* is from someone important…someone who knows. These pills come recommended from the finest experts in the land—true people of science. If I were going to stop taking them, I'd need to have some reason to doubt they work. But just look who has endorsed them!" He clicked on the TESTIMONIALS tab.

> "Finally, there's hope for the vertically challenged among us. I know of no better way to grow to be above six feet than Verticol. Reach for the stars. You just might grab one!" – Joelle Blarst, programming director, Mt. Kilowatt Medical Center

> "Consider me a Vertifan! Thanks, Dr. Hornswoggle, for standing up for all of us!" – Phelps McQuark, high-jump coach

> "These pills are a must-have for anyone serious about growing tall. But don't take my word for it. Try them yourself!"

— Dr. Donette Bridgefield, professor of physics, Haverton University

Hmm, thought Nia. *Something doesn't seem right.* But before she could speak, Gran added, "And you haven't even read the best one. Check this out!"

"As a top basketball player, I know a little something about being tall. That's why I invented Verticol with Dr. Hornswoggle. I want all of you to see what life is like from up this high." — Archibald 'Dr. Dunk' Swish

"And before you say anything," said Gran, "I know that 'Dr. Dunk' is just a nickname. They don't offer PhDs in dunking. Yet."

Nia knew she needed to put a stop to Gran's taking these pills—for his safety and for hers. And after reading, she knew just how to do it.

Nia thinks she can explain to Gran why the pills shouldn't be trusted. Can you?
Turn the page for a hint if you need it.

Hint from Nia

Gran is smart to look for expert sources he can trust, but just because someone claims to have expertise doesn't mean they actually are an expert. Online, people say they are experts all the time, both on websites and on social media. So we have to think carefully about whether they know what they're talking about. It's possible, after all, that the Verticol site has so much **bias** that it simply cannot be trusted. After all, it is trying to sell something.

One thing to consider: **Even if someone knows a lot about one topic, it doesn't mean they know a lot about other topics**. For example, a geologist is a scientist who studies the Earth. They may know a lot about things like volcanoes or rock formations, but they wouldn't necessarily know much about turtles. Or outer space. Or medicine!

Think a bit about Gran's experts. Are they the right people for the job?

Conclusion: Nia Clears the Air

Back in the kitchen, Nia sat at the table across from Gran. "First, Gran, can you tell me why you have a secret computer room?"

Gran shrugged innocently. "It's hardly a secret. You, Gram, and I all know…well, and whoever gave us this place. The elevator code was on the note we received telling us we'd won the apartment a year or so ago. Gram and I were out camping in Yosemite, and one morning we just found an anonymous postcard tucked into our tent flap. Said we won the apartment in a lottery and contained the deed and everything."

"And THAT didn't make you suspicious?" huffed Nia.

Gran paused and stroked his chin. "Well, it's funny. We didn't remember entering any lotteries, so that *was* odd. But you have to understand that your Gram and I are free spirits—almost opposite from how your mom came out. Our main questions were if the apartment had a hot tub (it does not) and if it had Wi-Fi (oh, baby, it does!). Beyond that, we thought trying to settle down a bit would be a new adventure. It's what got us talking about a visit with your mom!"

Nia thought that Gram and Gran really did sound like the opposite of her mom—and of her, for that matter. Who would want to move about, as they had? And who would be willing to move to a new apartment sight unseen, given by a total stranger? Nia preferred her world much more orderly, with rules to be followed and checklists to be checked. She was always surprised that more people didn't see things as she did.

Just then, Nia's nose reminded her that there were more pressing matters to attend to. "OK, Gran. Let's talk about these testimonials." As she spoke, Gram walked into the room and had a seat. She never missed an opportunity to see Gran change his mind. It was good exercise for him, she reckoned.

"Joelle Blarst is a programming director for a hospital, meaning she creates schedules but doesn't study or prescribe any pills. Does she have special expertise in medicine that qualifies her to tell you what you should do?"

"Well, no," said Gran. "I suppose she doesn't. But the testimonials are just to show the power of Verticol helping everyday people just like me!"

"That's true," said Nia. "But everyday people don't know everything, and they often think they know more than they do. Remember Constance B. Theymselves? Just because They Say something, doesn't make it true. For example, Phelps McQuark coaches high jump, but does that give him any special knowledge of the biology behind being tall?"

"I guess not," Gran chuckled.

"Right," said Nia. Even if McQuark probably works with tall people, that doesn't mean he understands anything about biology or medicine!"

"OK, they may not know about science, but what about

Doctor Bridgefield?" Gran said the "doctor" part really slowly—"Dooooccccctttttorrrr Bridgefield"—to make sure Nia didn't miss it. He was pretty sure he had her on this one.

But Nia was ready for him.

"Oh, yes. She's a doctor," she said.

"So, case closed," said Gran, folding his arms and grinning.

"Nuh-uh. Case open," said Nia. "Dr. Bridgefield is a physicist. Physicists study space and math and tiny particles and stuff. And that means she doesn't necessarily know much about medicine, right?"

"I guess not," said Gran slowly, his grin replaced by a look of mild anxiety. "But these pills were *invented* by Archibald 'Dr. Dunk' Swish, the tallest basketball player there is! He knows what it takes because he lives it every day! And he's famous!"

Nia took a deep breath. "Gran, just because someone is famous doesn't mean they know more than you. Dr. Dunk may be tall, but the pills didn't make him that way. He already *was* tall!"

"But…but…the MacGuffin Institute is studying this…" Gran was getting desperate.

"Sure," said Nia. "And maybe they'll find out that the pills *do* work. I don't think so, though. The MacGuffin Institute is owned by Dr. Hornswoggle, which means they have a big bias and probably aren't looking at the data fairly. And the trials are still ongoing, so we don't know the results."

"Ha-ha!" Gram cackled with delight. "She got you, Gran. Give up the ghost! Dr. Asmodeus P. Hornswoggle is nothing but a bloated wind-bag. And he's not the only one around here!"

But Gran didn't need any further encouragement. He was already spitting out the pills. "So much for another growth spurt, I suppose! C'mon, Nia. Help me get these to the toilet. It's a burial at sea for them!"

"You should never dump medicine in the toilet!" cried Gram behind them.

"But that's the thing," shot back Gran. "These *aren't* medicine! They're a scam!" With a great swoop of his arm, Gran dumped all his pills into the toilet and, in one great, gurgling flush, sent them off to the sewer. As they spiraled down, the colors created the most astonishing rainbow. Still holding their noses but now visibly less stressed, D'Angelo and Deja came in to cheer them off.

Later that day, a few blocks away, a manhole cover blew its lid. It was lifted by a geyser of frothing, bubbling rainbow water. No one could quite figure out what had caused it, but everyone agreed that the geyser had been extremely tall.

Chapter 6: Reliable Sources

"Can I grab your markers?" Deja asked, tugging at her sister's shirt.

"In the fridge," said Nia, without looking up from her book. A sound half like a cough and half like a snort came from D'Angelo's chair, where he was watching conspiracy videos, as usual.

"Refrigerating the markers makes for crisper colors," said Nia with an air of authority. "This lady on Craft RipRap does it."

D'Angelo made a show of rolling his eyes, lest Nia miss the gesture. "Do you believe *everything* you hear adults say?" he asked, looking down his nose and affecting a British accent as he spoke. If there was one thing he enjoyed, it was challenging Nia when he thought she was being ridiculous.

"Better than believing *nothing*, D," said Nia, with more than a bit of edge in her voice. If there was one thing she did *not* enjoy, it was being challenged by D'Angelo when she wasn't sure whether or not she was being ridiculous.

Deja ambled back to the room, her mouth full of markers.

"I wuv the cole markuz," she mumbled. "I kin put them in m'mout – like popsicles." She flashed a colorful grin and four markers fell to the floor.

"Gross," said Nia and D'Angelo simultaneously. Deja didn't hear them, though; she was hard at work. She had a species to save, after all.

* * *

"But we *have* to."

As far back as D'Angelo and Nia could recall, Deja always had a cause. Two years ago, it was buying local produce. Last month it was park beautification. Those at least made sense. But now it was…sharks.

She'd tried to explain this to Mom when they had their video call last night, but the reception had been so bad. Mom's Wi-Fi wasn't nearly as strong as theirs was in the Tower, and like usual, it was mostly garbled and frozen. "Sweetie…sounds good…brush teeth…bedtime… stupid Wi-Fi…" If Mom wasn't going to be able to help, she'd need to find other allies.

Deja had been lobbying Gram and Gran all morning to get them to invest in the program she found to help protect the shark population. She'd even made a poster for the campaign using Nia's markers, though Nia had said she could keep them since they'd been in her mouth. Already, the day was going her way.

The poster read, "SaVe OuR SHARKS," and was

punctuated with no fewer than seven exclamation points ("!!!!!!!"). Deja wanted to make sure her passion came through, since she really needed to win Gram and Gran to her side. Besides the remains of her allowance, she didn't have much money of her own, but Gram and Gran were old enough that she figured they must have something tucked away.

"You can see for yourself. Someone has to do something, and it can be us!" Deja held the laptop so close to Gram and Gran's faces that they both had to step back. On the screen, the site appeared in smooth professional lettering:

SaveOurSharks.com

Global Department of Aquatic Preservation – Urgent Bulletin

Friends, sharks are essential to the marine ecosystem, but most people don't look after them because they fear them. The shark population in the Dead Sea is the lowest it has ever been, and only your actions can help reverse this dangerous predicament.

Our team at the Global Department of Aquatic Preservation has been supporting sharks since May, and we stand ready to help nurture and support all the sharks we can locate in the endangered community. But we can't do it without you!

For $15 a month — just 50 cents a day — you can help us in this vital work. And if you act now, we'll send you a charm bracelet that reads, "I Stand with Sharks," so your friends will be inspired by your commitment, too. Please, friend, find it in your heart to act now. Don't let our planet's ecosystem collapse. Give sharks a fighting chance.

"I don't know," said Gran. "I had a school buddy who used to say, 'a penny saved is a penny earned,' and he was a right smart fella. Became an inventor, as I recall."

"Tell ya what, sweetie. Why don't you play with Nia and D'Angelo today, and your Gran and I will look into this," said Gram. "I think they mentioned something about an errand for the museum."

And with that, Gram and Gran leaned closer to the monitor, their faces awash in its pink and blue glow. D'Angelo and Nia didn't need much more of a cue than that. They were eager to get back into the town and continue exploring. "You coming, Marker Mouth?" D'Angelo called from the hallway.

Deja sighed dramatically and ran to catch up.

* * *

"This *should* be the address, but there's nothing here," said Nia, staring down at the scrap of paper Mr. Paperplate had given them. He'd tasked them with finding this Ruthbert person to let him know that the museum wouldn't be able to display the exhibits he submitted to be shown.

Just a few weeks earlier, Nia and D'Angelo had discovered

that Ruthbert's submissions—while they sounded true—were actually full of falsehoods. The kids had meant to go find this mystery man immediately. It's just that they'd actually been having a great time with Gram and Gran. Nia never would have thought family game night would be a fun use of time, but Gram and Gran invented their own diversions. They called them "challenges," and they were far better than anything the kids had done in Brooklyn. Last night's challenge was teaching the chickens to fly drones around the island using an interface one of their neighbors had designed. Deja won that one; it seemed she'd been spending a good deal of time on the rooftop.

("See? I told you chickens could fly!" Gram said.)

So, they really *had* meant to do Phineas's task immediately, but they'd been having so much fun with Gram and Gran that they kept putting it off.

Nia hoped this Ruthbert person wouldn't be too angry, but the truth was he wouldn't be much of anything if they couldn't find him.

"Don't you have GPS?" asked D'Angelo, who figured this beat being cooped up indoors. Gram and Gran may be odd, but at least they let him roam the town whenever he wanted. That's more than Mom ever did in Brooklyn.

Nia stared at her map program. According to it, they should be right on top of Ruthbert's address, but they weren't. They were just in the middle of some old stone bridge passing over a small stream. At least Deja was with them this time, as opposed to their trip to the museum.

"Why don't we ask those kids?" asked Deja, already walking up to three teens sitting on the bridge. Each kid sat with their legs dangling over the side and their face buried in their phone. Nia recognized them immediately, but before she could stop her sister, Deja was already trying to interact.

"Whatcha doin'?" Deja asked.

"I'm bored, so I'm posting about sitting on this bridge on social media," said Grind_Wizard.

"I'm bored, so I'm *reading* social media. This post is about three kids sitting on a bridge. I wish I got to do stuff like that. They're better looking *and* having a way more interesting time than we are," said Bugosaurus.

"I'm talking to you because you interrupted my social media time," said Duckle. "Any chance you could just message me any further questions?"

Deja began to respond when Nia interjected. "This is Grind_Wizard, Bugosaurus, and Duckle," she said. "Or at least, those are their screen names. They live here. They're the ones who helped us find the museum the other day."

"How was that, by the way?" mumbled Bugosaurus from behind his glasses and without looking up.

"Awesome," said Nia. "Awful," said D'Angelo. Both spoke at the same time, which made it sound more like "Awesomeful."

"Actually, that's why we're here," said Nia. "We need to locate a man named Ruthbert Rugglesford as a favor to the museum. He's supposed to live right here, but obviously, there's been a mistake. No one lives on a bridge."

"Ruthbert doesn't live *on* the bridge," said Duckle. "He lives *under* it." She pointed to a narrow footpath that wound its way beneath the bridge and led, as the kids would find out in a moment, to a surprisingly large, arched double door.

"Thanks!" Deja said though she received only a few grunts in response.

"Ahem," said Nia. "Thank you."

"Don't mention it," said Duckle. "Seriously, don't mention it. I don't think my followers would appreciate it if I were associated with out-of-towners."

* * *

"Well, they don't make bridges like this in Brooklyn," said D'Angelo, as he grabbed a large brass knocker that looked very much like a computer mouse. Before Nia could slow him down, he gave it three loud bangs. To his surprise, the door creaked open.

"This is some horror movie stuff," said D'Angelo as he began backing away, but before he could complete the thought, the kids were greeted with a scintillating display of colorful lights.

The walls of Ruthbert's house were covered in blue and purple neon, with tiny Christmas lights covering the ceiling. The lights were multi-colored crystal chandeliers, and the floor lit up wherever you stepped, making a pleasing "bloop" like a video game might as your character walked. For a house located under a bridge, everything was so… clean. Spotless, actually. Even the doormat looked like someone could eat off of it. It read "ENTER, but also RETURN."

"Helloooo?" called out Nia. "Mr. Rugglesford?" Instead of an answer, she got a series of video game noises and something that sounded a lot like a slot machine hitting the jackpot.

"Yo, what *is* this place?" asked D'Angelo as the three ventured further inside. The walls were a shiny, translucent plastic, except for a few places where it appeared they were wallpapered with some kind of technicolor bubble wrap.

Meanwhile, every door in Ruthbert's house was a different size, shape, and design, and all of them had bizarre labels. One triangle-shaped door said, "hot takes and hoaxes." Another, which looked like a pet door, said, "deep-fake cat videos." And another, a large keyhole-shaped opening, simply read, "meme assembly factory."

D'Angelo poked his head into an oval-shaped doorway labeled "AI hijinks" and saw the most curious thing: a wacky machine with a screen for a face and short, stubby legs clacking away at a keyboard. The machine was hard at work, its eyes narrowed in concentration as it carefully crafted its prose. As the machine wrote, its legs moved back and forth in a frenzied dance, its excitement and passion for artificial intelligence shining through in every word. And then, with a final flourish of its legs, the machine finished this very paragraph—yes, the one you are reading at this very moment—and stood up proudly, its screen glowing with pride.

"Nope. No way I can deal with this right now," said D'Angelo to himself, softly closing the door behind him. He caught up with his siblings a few paces down, by a large curtain, like something in an old-timey theater.

"Welcome, welcome!" came a voice from behind the curtain. It lifted up to reveal the strangest-looking man Nia and her siblings had ever seen.

Perhaps Ruthbert Rugglesford, a sallow string bean of a man somewhere in early middle age, could be forgiven for wearing a purple felt top hat, which had to be 150 years out of style (that is if it ever was *in* style). Perhaps his bowtie, which had pictures of bowties on it, was just a way of declaring his uniqueness. But his clothing made him hard to focus on for too long. Ruthbert wore a checkered button-down shirt, over which he wore another button-down shirt that was striped like some kind of carnival barker's uniform and covered in a not-insubstantial amount of glitter. His pants looked like a cross between a paper bag and a parachute.

"Hi, there," said Nia in a barely audible whisper. "Are you Mr. Rugglesford? Mr. Paperplate from the museum sent us. Um, we're really sorry, but…he wanted us to tell you that we couldn't display your exhibits. We're really sorry."

"Eh?" said the man in the top hat.

"We can't show your exhibits because they're full of

cheap lies," shouted D'Angelo, who was always eager to deliver some "real talk." Nia gave him a dirty look.

Ruthbert began to pace and scan the ground around his feet as though he were trying to find something he'd dropped. "Oh, dear. Oh, my."

"Like I said," gestured Nia, "we're really sorry. Maybe

we can hel—"

"It's just that those were some of my *very best* lies. I mean, I thought they were really good, undetectable even!"

"Wait, what?" asked D'Angelo.

"I chose things that people already believed. Those are the best kind, you know." Ruthbert held up one finger

and closed his eyes as though he were making a great pronouncement. "The best lies are the ones that people already believe are true."

Ruthbert snapped to, as if he suddenly realized he had company. "Forgive me, forgive me. I shall try harder next time," he said to the children with a wink.

"Umm…Mr. Ruthbert?" Nia asked, trying to be polite. "Don't you think maybe you should get some fact checkers to make sure you're accurate?"

"Fact Checkers?" Ruthbert scoffed. "My dear girl, I'm playing Fact Chess!"

Nia and D'Angelo had heard just about enough, but Deja couldn't help herself. "You know, Mr. Ruthbert, my mommy says it's never good to lie."

"Oh, sweet one, surely she's right. I don't want people to lie. All *I* want is for people to *believe*." As he said the word "believe," Ruthbert wiggled his fingers and made a sort of rainbow shape with his hands. Some glitter fell from his sleeve as he did this, creating an effect that, even D'Angelo had to admit, seemed pretty incredible.

"You see," said Ruthbert. "When I was your age, people said I could be anything I wanted to be. Did anyone ever tell you that?"

"Yes!" said Deja. "Sure," said Nia. "I guess," said D'Angelo.

"Right. Well, I wanted to be a dinosaur. Or a sonic boom. Or a ukulele. But when I said those things, they told me no.

And then I wanted to be the best football player in the country, but they said I couldn't do that either on account of I hate playing football. So you see, I'd been lied to. Swindled. Bamboozled. Hoodwinked."

Deja nodded. Ruthbert's logic was weird, but it also had a ring of truth.

"But then, one day, I found the internet." The lights in his house began to flash, and the jackpot noise sounded again at the mention of the word. "And here, I can be anything I want: a country lawyer who has won all his cases, a time-traveling golden retriever who solves mysteries, or a doctor who has invented pills that make people grow tall. You name it. Online, you can do it. You just have to get people to—" and again Ruthbert wiggled his fingers, "*believe.*"

"But you can't just say anything you want," said Nia, who felt like she was quickly becoming the most adult person in the room.

"Why not?" asked Ruthbert. "Free country, right? Besides, artificial intelligence can make any video or website look pristine and polished in seconds. No experience required! Tell me, what's something you've always wanted to be?"

"I'd like to be a tax collector," interjected Deja. No one quite knew where she'd come up with this idea or even if Deja knew what tax collectors did, but she said it with such conviction that Ruthbert's eyes twinkled.

"What's your name again?"

"Duckle," she said. Years of city living had made Deja too savvy to give her real name to a stranger. Later, she'd claim that Duckle was just the first name she could think of, but D'Angelo was certain it was revenge for the rude treatment she'd received earlier that day.

"Watch this, Duckle," Ruthbert said, opening a panel on one of the walls and typing a few commands into a screen. Suddenly, the theater curtains opened wider, and a giant screen lowered. Projected on the screen, a webpage appeared. "World's Best Tax Collection by Duckle," it read in shiny, animated font. Beneath the banner were five stars and the caption "No tax too small. 100% recommended."

"Wow!" said Deja. "I already have perfect reviews!"

"Yes, I 100% percent recommend your services. We believers need to stick together! Wink emoji."

Nia was exasperated. "First, no one says 'Wink emoji.' Second, you *can't* just put whatever you want online. You know that's not true. Dej—I mean Duckle—doesn't even have an accounting degree."

"Great point," said Ruthbert. He typed something more, and suddenly the site now read, "World's Best Tax Collection by Duckle, Certified Public Accountant."

Ruthbert beamed. "Congratulations, kid. You've just received your degree online! Double wink emoji!"

"But that's NOT the truth," said Nia.

"It's *my* truth," said Ruthbert with a grin. "Besides,

people make up things all the time online. I'll prove it. Who said, 'Prediction is difficult, especially about the future?'"

Nia and D'Angelo looked this up on their phones while Deja used a computer terminal that jutted out from a nearby wall. As they did, Ruthbert said something strange, as if he was speaking to other people who weren't in the room. "If you're reading this at home, why don't you try too? Look up who said that quote. How many different people does the internet tell you? The kids and I will be here when you get back."

* * *

After a few moments passed, the kids looked up. "I got the physicist Niels Bohr," said Nia. "Nostradamus, the French astrologer," said D'Angelo. "Yogi Berra?" asked Deja, pronouncing the famous baseball player's name more like "Yogi Bear-ah."

"Exactly," said Ruthbert. "Most people just say whatever they want, and they rarely fact-check. Information moves fast— like a superhighway. No one has time to read the road signs or check if they're actually pointing in the right direction."

"That's why I don't trust *anything*," said D'Angelo.

"Works for me," said Ruthbert. "If you think everything is a lie, then everything might be true, too. It's all the same. For example, I can make a page claiming the moon landing didn't happen, and you'll believe it."

"But it *didn't* happen," D'Angelo replied. This was one of his very favorite conspiracy theories, partly because the idea of anyone actually walking on the moon seemed crazy but mostly because it annoyed Nia.

"OK, so I'll make a page that says it *didn't* happen, and you'll think *that's* a lie because you don't believe anything."

D'Angelo was frustrated. Ruthbert had a point. If he didn't believe *anything*, then there would be no way to know the truth when he found it. "Fine, then how do you know if something is the real deal?"

"Oh, don't worry. People are way too lazy for that. Why, first, they'll have to slow down when they see surprising or new information. That alone is usually more than anyone wants to do. People can be so wonderfully careless! And even if they do slow down, they'll have to actually look at the source of their information and decide if it *is* believable."

"OK," said Nia, "But at least we can trust some sites right off the bat, like .orgs. They're organizations, so you know you can count on them."

"That's the best part!" cried Ruthbert with joy. "It's easy to get a '.org' website—just about anyone can get one. Adults think it makes the site special, but it doesn't! People need to do their own research, but they never do."

"What do you mean by 'research'?" asked D'Angelo.

"You know, like investigating the source. If the group is an organization, do they have a bias? If it's a publication, do they have a track record of honesty? Can you find a different trustworthy source that confirms what the site says?

Basically, any time you are looking at a website or video that feels surprising, you *shoooould* pause and think about whether you really know and trust the source, and look them up if you don't know."

"Well, at least you can trust universities and the government," said Nia, crossing her arms.

"Maybe," said Ruthbert. "It's true there's a lot of great research on university sites. And you can usually trust the government for boring stuff like where to get your driver's license or what day the trash is picked up. But here's the thing. There are *a lot* of groups with websites that end in .gov or .edu, and not all of them care about getting things right. Sometimes their own goals are what they care about most. So, while in *theory* a government or a university has a strong incentive *not* to lie, you can't totally accept what they say without doing more research—especially when they're talking about controversial issues. Many politicians are grade-A fibbers— heart emoji!—and universities employ people with lots of ideas… some of them wonderfully bad!"

Ruthbert stared off into the distance for a moment. "Note to self," he said aloud. "Found Rugglesford University and hire the world's greatest liars as professors or…" he turned to the children, "how does Senator Rugglesford sound?"

"It—" started D'Angelo, but Ruthbert was already answering his own question: "I like it. It sounds *trustworthy*."

"So, we have to research sources no matter what type of

site they're on," Nia said.

Ruthbert rolled his eyes. "But who has time for looking things up? Bored barf emoji."

Nia ignored that last part. She was furiously making a checklist of the things Ruthbert was saying, even though he didn't realize he was helping them. So far she had:

- ☑ *check organizations for bias; research your sources (even .gov, .edu, and .org)*
- ☑ *look for trusted others to confirm what site says*

She decided to play dumb, hoping to pump him for more information. "But lots of sites are '.com,'" she said. "They're commercial. Or they're just someone's blogs or videos."

Ruthbert chuckled. "Those are my favorites. Sites that are trying to sell you something say up front that their *goal* is to get you to spend money, but most people believe them like they were gospel. Their whole purpose is to convince you to fork over cash!"

"And blogs?" Ruthbert continued. "I mean, maybe an expert's blog is OK, but how many of your friends are checking the things they write online? Most people have the goal of *sounding* smart; very few do the work to *be* smart."

Nia added to her list:

- ☑ *beware sites trying to sell something*
- ☑ *double-check blogs + social media videos if not an expert*

"This sounds like a lot," said D'Angelo.

"It is!" cried Ruthbert. "Once you've been reading long enough, you start to get a better sense of who you can trust and who you can't. But most people skip those steps when they're your age, which means they grow up to be adults who will believe anything. And those are my favorite people! It's far more fun and far less work to get them to believe whatever it is they see, like," and he said this next part with great flourish, "*magic!*"

Ruthbert threw more glitter into the air. The computer noises in his house whirred and bleeped with glee.

"Most of my fortune comes from the kind donations of *believers* out there. I just make up a cause that sounds important, and I make a webpage. And then people who want to give away their money just *believe* what I say and send it to me! Everyone wins! They *believe* they did something good, and I *believe* I will enjoy spending their money. It's a win-win situation. My latest site is all about saving sharks. Let's see if I can make some money with it, shall we?"

Deja took on a pale hue. Could this be the same site she'd brought to Gram and Gran this morning? It didn't feel possible. That page was clean, polished, and looked letter-perfect. But she glanced up at Nia, who was already dialing Gram and Gran's number on her phone.

"Heya, kiddo. What's the matter?" Gran asked over speakerphone.

"Gran! Gram! Whatever you do, don't give money to that sharks group. It's—"

"A scam?" interjected Gran. "Of course, kiddo. After that fiasco with the tallness pills, we decided to sharpen our wits. We saw it was hogwash a mile away."

Gram and Gran knew the sharks site was a hoax, but how?
Turn the page for a hint.

Hint from Gram and Gran

The trick online is to figure out what's more likely to be trustworthy and what's less likely. We've already learned the value of looking for bias and reading laterally to see if a source or its claims are credible. Besides that, there are a few moves you can use to keep your radar alert for sneaky sites.

What can you look for? Go back to look at the list Nia made from Ruthbert's ramblings. Here's what she wrote:

- ☑ check organizations for bias; research your sources (even .gov, .edu, and .org)
- ☑ look for trusted others to confirm what the site says
- ☑ beware of sites trying to sell something
- ☑ double-check blogs + social media videos if not an expert

Then, apply that checklist to the website Deja showed Gram and Gran. How many things can you find that make the site seem untrustworthy?

Conclusion: Gram and Gran Catch a Big One

"First of all," said Gram, who had grabbed the phone from her husband, "there's no such thing as The Global Department of Aquatic Preservation. It sounds like a government agency, but we checked, and that's not real."

"Besides," interjected Gran, not to be outdone, "the site is a '.com.' It's clearly trying to sell us things, so we know we need to be especially careful about believing it. What kind of government site would try to ask for money or sell merchandise?"

"So," added Gram, "we looked up sharks and the Dead Sea. It's true that they're 'endangered' there, but that's because no sharks actually live in the Dead Sea!"

Ruthbert's eyes darted back and forth like he'd just figured something out. "I'm sorry. Did you say you're Gram and Gran…of the penthouse at the all-the-way, very-very, tippy top of the Tower?"

"Yes. Who's this?" asked Gram.

"Ruthbert Rugglesford, at your service!" he cried. "And I want to thank you and your grandchildren for exposing the weaknesses in this site. I'll have it removed at once. In fact, I'll need to make this up to you and your lovely family."

If Gram or Gran were concerned with Ruthbert's scheme, their voices didn't betray it. "Ruthbert? Why, you're the young man we keep seeing taking photos around the Tower."

"Indeed!" Ruthbert cried. "I've always wanted to take a

tour, you see."

"Well, then, you simply must come by. And thank you for taking such good care of our grandkids." Nia, D'Angelo, and Deja all shot each other glances.

"Now, what is it you do for a living?"

"A little bit of everything," Ruthbert said with a wink. "Got my degree online, after all."

Chapter 7: Gone Phishing

"We have a bit of paddling to do, so how about we play a game while we wait?"

Against Nia's better judgment, she, D'Angelo, and Deja found themselves in a boat with Ruthbert, who, having explained that the shark website was a misunderstanding, had offered to take the children fishing to make up for it. D'Angelo, having always wanted to learn, jumped in to agree before Nia could express reservation. Deja, who still appreciated that Ruthbert had made her a tax collector, had also enthusiastically nodded. It looked like Nia would have to tag along to make sure nothing weird happened.

So far, at least, things seemed normal. Gran and Gram had waved goodbye to them at the dock, and the four of them had climbed into a small, wooden rowboat with a trunk of supplies at the end. Ruthbert had insisted each of them wear life jackets, which annoyed D'Angelo but calmed Nia a bit. The cool, salty air felt comforting against her skin, and the rhythmic paddling of the oars gave her a sense of security. It sounded like Ruthbert was playing a game with Deja, which was nice. Maybe the day at the bridge really *had* been a misunderstanding.

"How about 'I Spy?'"

"I love that game!" said Deja. "I'll go first. I spy something made of wood."

"The rowboat?" asked Ruthbert.

"Yes! Your turn!"

"Oh, good! By the way, what type of computer do your Gram and Gran use?"

"Oh, it's a CompuSoft. I really like it."

"Thanks! OK, back to the game. I spy something that begins with an F."

Deja scanned the horizon. All she saw was a bunch of water. "Is it fish?"

"Nope! Sorry! But do you want another guess?"

"Yes, please."

"OK. That'll be one dollar. Just write down your mom's credit card number, and we can charge it."

"Wait. Why do I have to pay a dollar?"

"It's called an in-game purchase! You can pay to enhance your experience!"

"But 'I Spy' is free!"

"Yes, it totally is. But wouldn't you like to have even more fun? Tell you what. For two more dollars, I'll give you three extra guesses and an invisible rainbow cloak."

"Oooh! I love rainbows…almost as much as unicorns!"

"Well, then," snorted Ruthbert, "you're in luck. The invisible cloak is *also* covered in unicorns!"

Nia, who had been half listening until then, jumped in. "That's all right, Ruthbert," she snapped. She turned to her sister: "Day, I think we've had enough 'I Spy.'"

Ruthbert shrugged. "I think we've reached the spot, anyway. Let's do this! Oars up!" D'Angelo and Nia pulled their paddles out of the water. By this point, they were far enough from Barnaby's Corner that the island looked tiny, like some chin hair sticking out on the horizon. "If we're going to do this, we'll need equipment," he said as he opened the large trunk at the end of the boat.

"I'll take the longest rod!" shouted D'Angelo, reaching out his hands.

"A rod?" chuckled Ruthbert. "That won't help at all. If you want to go phishing, you'll need *this*," he said, handing each child a sleek black laptop.

"I don't understand," said Deja. "I thought you said we were going fishing."

"Oh no, child!" said Ruthbert. "I'm personally against killing for sport. It's so barbaric. Is that what your siblings thought we were doing?"

"Yes. Nia and D'Angelo both said so."

"No, no... we're going *phishing*!" he said. "P-h-i-s-h-i-n-g."

D'Angelo scoffed. "Dude. Phishing is when you trick people into giving you their passwords or credit card information to take their money." He crossed his arms. "Not cool."

"That's right! It's the *hot* new thing on the internet, and I want to get a piece of the action. I took us out here where we'll be on a different Wi-Fi without anyone seeing what we're up to."

"Ruthbert," said Deja firmly, "this sounds wrong. I've been warned there are lots of mean, nasty people on the internet who want to take everyone's money."

"Oh, that sounds terrible," said Ruthbert. "You need to watch out for mean and nasty people, for sure. But I'm a

fun-loving and friendly person, so when I take everyone's money, it'll be totally different!"

"What would you even do with it?" asked D'Angelo defiantly.

"I don't know. I'd probably use it to buy a bank. That'd be like getting a wish and then wishing for more wishes. Pretty smart, eh?"

D'Angelo thought it actually sounded fairly clever, but Nia was having none of it. "That's not how banks work, Ruthbert."

"Eh? Well, I was always much better at the scheming part. I'll keep at it once I have the money. But today, I'm not after money. I'm after a password—a special password that will get me access to the greatest computer ever built."

D'Angelo shrugged, and as he did, Ruthbert finished typing something on his own computer. "And… sent!"

"What did you send?" asked Nia.

"Just a note to your Gram and Gran, to see if I can gain access to that secret room!"

"Wait, what?" panicked Nia.

"I just phished for their password! I think I'll get it. Won't that be fun?"

"Huh? What is he talking about? What secret room?" asked Deja. D'Angelo, for his part, was busy trying to see if

his laptop had games on it.

"Nothing—" Nia blurted, her face turning bright red. Had Ruthbert invited them out here as a trick? He honestly didn't seem that clever. Still, Nia was pretty sure the computer room Gran had shown her was top secret. She hadn't even talked to D'Angelo and Deja about it yet. And now they were in the middle of the ocean with no way for her to warn her sweet, unsuspecting grandparents.

* * *

"Mail call!" shouted Gram. She did that every time she and Gran received an email. They shared an address—and while most people would have found it annoying, Gran said it reminded him of his time in the army. The kids could never figure out which war he'd fought in. "I told them, 'No sir. I absolutely won't fire a gun,'" Gran had said and puffed up his chest. "But I *did* fire up the grill and was known for having the best beef goulash this side of the Atlantic. Won me a green star."

Gran jumped out of his Thinking Chair. He'd been *thinking* about taking a nap in it, and then—as if by magic—it had happened. Now, he was moving swiftly to Gram and the computer to see what they'd received.

"Oh dear," said Gram. "It seems we may have a computer virus!" She pointed to the email title, which read, "Caution! Your computer may be infected with viruses."

"Huh. Better check it out, Gram."

She opened the email. Here's what it read:

From: CompuSoft Headquarters <viruses_team@comppusoft.com.gz>

Subject: Caution! Your computer may be infected with viruses

Dear Gram and Gran,

This is to inform you that your computer may have been infected with viruses. Our offices have detected this threat and wish to clean your computer so that it will not be having problems. Your assistance is kindly requested.

To support you click on <this link> and enter the password to your secret computer room. From there, our technician can fix all problems with zero cost for you the consumer. In fact, because you are a loyal customer, we also want to let you know that you have won much money in our sweepstakes. Simply share your password at <this link> to claim your prize. We are certain that Nia, D'Angelo, and Duckle will all enjoy a free computer and money for college.

Thank you for you help in this urgent matter,

CompuSoft HQ

"Hmm," said Gran. "What do you think? Should we give them our password?"

"Oh, stop it, you kidder. You know as well as I do that this is a scam. I can spot at least three signs that this email isn't trustworthy," chuckled Gram.

"I can see four!" said Gran.

"Hmm. Come to think of it, there are five. Yes, five signs that this is a hoax email. Besides, everyone knows you shouldn't click on a link in an email when you don't know the sender. It's just someone trying to get your information. That should be a crime."

"I think it *is* a crime," said Gran. "But it happens so often people don't even notice it anymore. I hope our grandkids are smart enough to spot this stuff. You know these are just going to get harder and harder to catch as scammers get better at it."

Gram and Gran found at least five reasons to doubt this email. Can you?
Turn to the next page for a hint.

Hint from Gram

Like I said, you should *never* **click on links in an email where you don't recognize the sender**. Even when I *do* recognize them, I'm careful to avoid this if possible. For example, if my bank wants me to go their website, I can just open my browser and get there myself. It's always better to find the site yourself than take the shortcut since that shortcut might take you to a site designed to steal your information.

In general, it's smart to read emails on the defense—especially if they ask you to click something. There are lots of folks out there trying to steal information from us by getting us to click on things and share passwords and credit card information. This is known as **phishing**. Once they have your information, they can do all types of damage or steal from you.

Sometimes, even, the senders have done some snooping and learned something about you in hopes of making the email appear more trustworthy. They might know, for example, that you use CompuSoft or have three grandkids. This is even sneakier, and it's called **spear phishing**. The sender usually tries to impersonate someone you trust to get you to let your guard down.

This email has several signs it wasn't written by the "CompuSoft Virus Team" or whoever it's claiming to be from. Read it again slowly. Can you spot things that don't make sense, even if you're not sure why? Does anything not sound right to you?

Conclusion: No Cookies for Scammers

"Let's rattle off what we found," said Gram, already hitting the "report" button in her email and then deleting the letter. The two shuffled over to the kitchen for an afternoon nosh.

"First, it's true we use CompuSoft, but I've never heard of a whole headquarters just emailing a single user. That feels strange to me, and anytime something feels strange, I pause and think twice."

"And did you see that email address?" asked Gran as he brought out a jar of huckleberry marmalade and some kale crackers. "It doesn't look like any company email address I've ever seen, and it spells CompuSoft incorrectly!"

"Good catch," nodded Gram, pouring each a cup of hot coriander tea. "A misspelling is a huge sign this is a fake. Besides, the tone of the whole thing just feels off to me. The letter says the computer may be infected with 'viruses.' That's so vague and unclear, like someone is making it up. And the grammar is just plain *off* in a few sentences."

"Well, at least they were polite," Gran said. "Not enough of that these days, especially in thieves."

"Mmm-hmm," Gram nodded, biting into a thick piece of a pistachio-rhubarb fritter she'd baked earlier that morning.

"Could you imagine, though? What if we'd won computers for the kids and all that money? That'd have been so nice," Gran said.

"If there's one thing I've learned," said Gram as she patted the corner of her mouth with a napkin, "it's that there's no such thing as free money. Telling me I've won money is a total giveaway. The scammer did know we have three grandkids, though, which is disturbing."

Gram paused. A look of worry suddenly fell across her face. "That gets me thinking, didn't you and I accept *this* apartment from a random note left on the flaps of our tent?"

"That was the *old* us," said Gran confidently. "After that Verticol debacle, we're practically unscammable! And I think I know who is targeting us, too. Pretty sure this is Ruthbert. That man has just an insane sense of humor."

"I think so," Gram replied. "He's trying to get into that computer room. But the note when we moved in said we couldn't show it to anyone but family. I plan to give that young man a stern talking to, I do!"

"Indeed," said Gran, his mouth now full of Ms. Ramekin's extra crispy chocolate-bacon-jalapeno-cheddar-gorgonzola poppers. He was glad he and Gran had stopped back to purchase a box for the house, though he'd admonished Ms. B for her unkind treatment of Le Petit Café earlier. "Besides, Ruthbert didn't even get all our information right. Why in the world would he think Deja's name is Duckle?"

Gran and Gram continued about this way for the better part of the afternoon until it was time to pick the kids up at the dock. D'Angelo and Deja looked like they'd enjoyed the sun, but Nia looked so worried.

"Did you guys receive any emails today?" she'd asked.

"Oh, no. Nothing but scams," Gram said, to Nia's relief.

Each of the kids was treated to a chocolate popper, though when Ruthbert put out his hand, Gram said, "Oh, sorry, Ruthbert. Only people who don't run scams get a cookie."

Deja put her hands on her hips. "Yeah, Ruthbert. No cookies for scammers," she said. Her mouth was so full, though, it sounded more like "nohkookiesfuhscammas."

D'Angelo made a sad trombone sound: *Womp, womp*.

Ruthbert seemed undeterred. "I'm sorry, kids! We'll get them next time! You know what they teach in school, you just have to keep trying when you want something."

"That's a good lesson," shrugged Gran, and gave Ruthbert a cookie for helping teach the kids.

"It certainly is," said Gram. And the group walked back to the Tower.

Chapter 8: Cherry Picking

"Do you know Mr. Rugglesford?" Nia had asked Phineas when the invitation to go cherry picking first came a few days ago. After the disaster that phishing had turned out to be, he had offered to take them to the island's cherry orchard to make up for it. He had even invited Phineas to join them.

"Not at all," Phineas had said, "but he seems to know me. At least, he acts like he does. And the cherry orchard is a wonderful place. Barnaby's Corner is famous for its cherries."

"I'm pretty sure cherries can't grow in this climate," D'Angelo said.

"Well, yes. That's why they're famous," Phineas responded. "It's a miracle that they're here at all!"

Everything seemed set for a typical summer activity with absolutely no tomfoolery involved.

But on the morning of the trip, just as they were about to leave, Phineas had arrived, his face red and sweaty, breathing hard. "Sorry, kids," he began. "Can't go with you. Huge news story breaking. Biggest of the year. It's all hands on deck down at the Barnaby Star. Or all *hand* on deck, since I'm the only reporter."

"Wow!" said Deja. "What is it, Mr. Paperplate? A volcano? An alien landing?"

Phineas's eyes flashed. "Bigger! The town council just voted three to two to allow a variance to local ordinance 13.6A!"

"What?" D'Angelo asked.

"Being pretty much the center of the internet, Barnaby's Corner gets all the new memes first. And, of course, because they're so fresh, people love using them. About twenty years back, all the businesses on the island started using memes in all their advertisements and on all their storefronts. Most folks thought they made the town look hideous, but they just couldn't stop using them," Phineas said.

"Uh, what's a meme again?" asked Deja.

"It's those little images Mom uses when she texts her friends," D'Angelo said. "They're like inside jokes, but everyone gets them and riffs on them. Adults love them."

"Sure do!" interjected Phineas. "And that was part of the problem. Adults here would put up the newest memes, and then a little while later, they'd have to take them down when even newer ones popped up. The place was littered with old posters and billboards. So the town council passed a law saying that the only memes you could use were ones on a special list. And they NEVER update the list. We've been stuck with I Can Haz Cheezburger? and Dancing Baby for decades!"

"What are you talking about?" asked Nia.

"I don't know! I don't know what they mean anymore! Nobody does. BUT the council just approved a new one for the first time!"

"Cool!" said D'Angelo. "What is it?"

Phineas paused dramatically. "RACECAR CRAB TAKES THE FLAG."

"And what does that mean?"

"We won't know what it means until people start using it. And that's where I come in. I have to interview everyone about it to determine what it means." He pulled out a notebook and looked at them thoughtfully. "So what do *you* think 'racecar crab takes the flag' means?"

"It's a trick," said D'Angelo. "It doesn't mean anything."

"A crab driving a racecar is funny," Deja said.

"A crab driving a racecar is funny *because* it doesn't mean anything," said Nia.

Ruthbert cleared his throat. "To 'take the flag' means to win a race. Crabs ambulate—err, walk—sideways. If a crab is in a racecar, the racecar will go sideways instead of forwards. It should not be able to win the race going sideways. So, if racecar crab wins the race, then that's a surprising success from doing something in a very different way. That's what I think it means. It means 'a surprising thing happened because someone did something differently than usual.'"

"Nah," said D'Angelo.

"Doubt it," said Nia.

"Doesn't make sense to me," said Deja.

Phineas made a final mark in his notebook and put it back in his pocket. "In any case," he said, "I must be off! My apologies, Mr. Rugglesford. Kids, be good, and pick some cherries for me." Then he dashed away.

* * *

"Did I promise you something stupendous or what?" asked Ruthbert as he held out his hands and spun around.

Now that they were in the orchard, Nia had to admit it was beautiful, just as Ruthbert had promised. Thousands of cherry bunches hung just above their heads, glistening in the summer sun. Maybe cherry picking wasn't such a bad idea after all. Gram and Gran had seemed to feel this would be good exercise. And the cherries themselves were incredible. She'd been plucking them off trees to share with D'Angelo and Deja as the group explored. And yet…

Something just felt off about Ruthbert. The clothing thing still weirded her out. Who wore a button-down shirt on top of another button-down shirt? Or a top hat, for that matter?

"This is nice, Ruthbert. Just remember, you promised Gram and Gran no phishing."

"Of course! Of course! Besides, we're not even in a boat, so how could we possibly…"

At this point, Nia figured, there wasn't much use in trying to explain what she meant. She and D'Angelo had spent

more than a few nights after Deja's bedtime trying to size up Ruthbert, and they were still stumped. Sure, Gram and Gran seemed to think he meant well, but they'd come to realize Gram and Gran weren't exactly grounded in reality.

"Well, I think this is wonderful," said Deja. "Just make sure we don't do anything *villainous*." Deja had learned another new word and was trying to use it everywhere. There had been a small incident that morning when she described Gram's breath as having a distinctly *villainous* scent.

Ruthbert paused as if deciding whether to share something. "You know, you shouldn't speak about villains that way," he said, with a slight air of haughty frustration.

"Gimme a break," said D'Angelo.

"Oh, take all the breaks you need! Just don't take it out on villains," said Ruthbert. "Why, some of the most successful world leaders are villains! And not just that. Many of the most beloved celebrities and businesspeople and innovators are villains, one and all."

Deja hadn't really thought about it that way. She looked to her brother, who was opening his mouth to protest when Ruthbert continued.

"History is positively teeming with villains; some of them have even written the history books! Why, if you think about it, most villains are the heroes of their own stories, just with their own…unique ideas for how to make the world better."

"Yeah," said D'Angelo, "for *themselves*."

"Well," sniffed Ruthbert, "They say that charity begins at home."

Deja's ears perked up. She thought of Constance B. Theymselves and her yappy dog.

"Anyhow, I'll have you know that I'm the president of the VSBW, the Villainous Society for a Better World. We're a small group—really just me right now—but I was hopeful you three would join! And members all get a free tube of the toothpaste I invented, 'Ruthbert's Ruby-Juice Tooth-Pampering Serum.'"

"You invented a toothpaste?" asked Deja, genuinely interested. She'd never met an inventor before, and toothpaste was one of those magical things that everyone used but didn't really know much about.

"You betcha!" Ruthbert clapped. "Ruby-Juice Tooth-Pampering Serum is consistently named the best-tasting toothpaste this side of the Grand Canyon. And it's dentist recommended!"

"Perhaps I can try it after cherry picking?" asked Deja.

"Well, of course you can," Ruthbert smiled kindly. "So, let me show you how to do it. First things first, you'll probably want to put down that fruit. I said we were going cherry *picking*, not cherry *eating*. And cherry *picking* is something you do with facts."

Deja was so confused. Weren't cherry picking and cherry eating basically the same thing? How could she cherry pick a fact? And why did Nia suddenly look so upset?

"You see," said Ruthbert, "Facts are like cherries. Some are sweet and juicy, while others are sour and flat. So, when I make an argument, I always make sure I cherry pick only the sweet, juicy facts I like—and not the ones that disprove my case. That's what people mean when they say you're cherry picking your evidence."

D'Angelo was intrigued. He remembered hearing a basketball announcer say something about cherry picking players' statistics a few months ago, but he'd ignored it at the time. Perhaps, finally, Ruthbert was showing them a useful skill?

"Can you show us an example?"

"Actually, I already have," said Ruthbert. "My toothpaste!"

"Wait," said Nia. "Did you lie to us?"

"Of course not, Nia. Why ever would I lie? I just chose the best facts. The finest ones, indeed. For example, I told you that Ruby-Juice toothpaste won taste tests. And it did! But that's because it's made of 100% straight sugar. That's why everyone loves the flavor so much!"

"Hang on," said D'Angelo. "You also said it was dentist-recommended. Why would dentists recommend that?" D'Angelo thought of his many trips to Dr. Singh, who was always filling his cavities and trying to convince him to eat less sugar. Maybe D'Angelo would have to send Dr. Singh a tube of Ruby-Juice toothpaste to get him off his back.

"Whoa, whoa, whoa," protested Ruthbert. "I said it

was *dentist* recommended, not *dentists* recommended." He emphasized the final "s" in "dentists."

"My cousin is a dentist, and I promised to stop singing outside his house at three o'clock in the morning if he recommended my brand. So, you see, everything I told you was 100% true! *That's* cherry picking!"

Nia was uncomfortable. Even if Ruthbert hadn't lied, this definitely didn't feel honest. "Ruthbert, isn't it deceptive to not share all the relevant facts about something? I mean, you didn't quite lie, but you weren't quite truthful either."

"Oh, but those other facts are *terrible*, just terrible. They don't help me at all," Ruthbert said. "For example, a study found that my toothpaste actually causes 95% more cavities than any other brand. In fact, it's far, far worse than just forgetting to brush! One of the researchers even called it 'tooth rotting gel.' Those facts won't help my case, so I just close my eyes, wriggle my nose, and—poof!—I pretend like they don't exist!"

Following that sentence, Ruthbert leapt into what only could be described as a bit of a jig, at least as performed by someone who didn't really know what jigs were supposed to look like. He hopped on one foot, then another, then clicked his heels as he sang this song:

Don't you worry, don't feel blue,
If the odds look bad to you.
Make your case and make it stick,

When the facts you cherry pick.

D'Angelo smacked his forehead with his palm. "There is something wrong with this guy, for sure." But Ruthbert continued merrily along.

No need to fib, lie, or deceive,
Just cherry pick and they'll believe.
A challenge, kids, I will allow:
Name anything, I'll show you how!

"Oh, Mr. Ruthbert, you're not so sneaky after all!" Deja said. "You're showing us how all your tricks work!"

Ruthbert's face turned dark. "You take that back," he said. "I'll have you know that sharing these secrets is *exactly* what makes me a great villain! Because here's the thing—even when adults know about these traps, they still fall into them! Every time! The more confident they are that they can't be fooled, the easier it is to trick them! That's why I love the internet so much. No one in the history of the internet has ever thought they were wrong about *anything*!"

Nia was out-and-out revolted by the idea of cherry picking. What an unscrupulous way of convincing people to agree with you! She was determined to stop Ruthbert at his own game. "Fine," she said, "You issued a challenge. I accept, and I choose climate change." Nia had done her eighth-grade capstone project on climate change, and she fancied herself a bit of an expert on the topic. For example, she knew 97% of scientists agreed global warming was happening *and* was caused by people. At least, that's what the U.S. government reported the month she gave the report.

"Oh, that's too easy!" said Ruthbert.

"Try me," said Nia. She'd proudly received an A on that project, which in her reckoning was more like four A's since the rest of her group let her do most of the work. That had been frustrating, but she figured that decades from now when she was a famous researcher, and they were fetching her iced lattes or whatever famous researchers drank, the score would be settled.

"Fine! Here's my case:

- First, you claim the climate is changing, but the climate has changed in years past. That's just what climates do! In fact, a good number of scientists say this has nothing to do with human activity. It's just how things are! I'm happy to get you a quote from any of them. I can think of at least a dozen who say that!
- Second, last week was very cold, and it's summer. Remember that day we all wore sweatshirts? If the Earth is heating up, I don't see any proof of it.
- Finally, come to think of it, last winter it snowed five times! The weather in Barnaby's Corner was the coldest in decades. You can look it up! So 'global warming' is pretty much bunk."

Nia paused for a moment. She knew that Ruthbert was doing his best to trick her, so now she had to point out how his cherry-picked arguments weren't worth much.

Nia thinks she can name the flaws in Ruthbert's arguments.
Can you?
Turn the page for a hint.

Hint from Nia

Ruthbert is **cherry picking** his facts, and we need to call him out on this. I already learned a few facts from researching my school report that might help here, so go back and read the paragraph that described what I learned.

Then, think a little bit about the facts Ruthbert has presented. Even if they *are* true, how might they only show a small sliver of the picture? For example, Ruthbert mentions the local weather during a single week or season, but that only represents a small period of time. Perhaps go online and look up global heat trends over the past few years or decades. If you check independent, credible sites, you're most likely to come up with more comprehensive, accurate data to contrast with Ruthbert's cherry-picked facts. Think of it like building a web. Your web of information will always be stronger than Ruthbert's—or anyone's—cherry-picked strands.

Conclusion: Ruthbert Tastes the Bitter Truth

Ruthbert continued to dance his strange jig, hopping from one foot to the other.

"No need to fib, lie, or deceive,

Just cherry pick, and they'll believe."

"Ruthbert, did you say you found a dozen scientists who agree with your view?"

"I sure did!" he cried with glee.

"Well, that may seem like a lot, but there are *thousands* of scientists out there, and 97% agree with my view. It feels like you just found a few random people who happened to agree with you and ignored all the rest."

Ruthbert paused mid-hop. "Yes, that's just what I did. So what?"

"Well," said Nia, "that makes your case sound much stronger than it is. In fact, most scientists think you're wrong. When I listen to arguments that mention researchers, I often ask what the scientific consensus is." Sensing Deja's question before she even asked it, Nia said: "Deja, *consensus* is when almost everyone agrees with something."

"Yeah," said D'Angelo. "Like, the *consensus* is that Ruthbert can't dance!"

This was all Deja needed. She continued her stroll around the orchard accompanied by her new word: "The *consensus* is that cherries taste good on ice cream. The family *consensus* is that I'm the cutest child."

Meanwhile, Nia resumed her showdown with Ruthbert.

"D, do you remember Ruthbert's other arguments?"

"Yeah," said D'Angelo. "He said that because it was cold last week and last year here, climate change wasn't happening."

Ruthbert perked up. "That's right! I picked those facts fresh just for this argument. They totally support my point."

"Perhaps," said Nia. "But the thing is, those are tiny, single data points. I happen to have seen the government's research on global temperature, and the numbers around the planet have been steadily climbing for years. Even if one small place has a cold week or a cold season, that doesn't mean the planet isn't warming overall. Your data is just too small to matter. You chose it because it made you look correct, even though you know you're not!

"Got me again, friend!" cried Ruthbert with joy. "But that's the whole point! When people cherry pick, they *know* they have a weak case. That's why we do it!"

This got Deja's attention. "Why, that's positively *villainous*," she said.

Ruthbert froze. He closed his eyes and exhaled for what felt like a full minute. Then, from deep within him came what sounded like a cross between a sniffle and a whimper.

Wiping more than one tear from his cheek, Ruthbert affectionately pulled Deja in for a hug. "That's the loveliest thing anyone has said this whole week. I *knew* you'd understand me!"

At this point, Nia was convinced. There was something deeply, deeply wrong with this man…though she couldn't help but think Ruthbert was the friendliest villain she could imagine.

Chapter 9: Conspiracies A Go-Go

One thing was for certain, this was a problem for the Great Thinking Chair.

In the corner of his study was an overstuffed brown recliner that Gran always returned to when he had a difficult problem to solve. Ironically, Gran spent very little time in the chair itself. He usually hopped up and paced around it in circles as he pondered. As a result, the chair appeared in almost mint condition, while the rug around it was worn from many evenings of worry and thought, like the rings of a tree. Today he was adding a few more.

Gram was out with Nia and Deja for a "girls' day"—whatever that meant—and Gran's time with D'Angelo was going down in flames. It all began that morning when D'Angelo asked him about his travels. Gran had shown him pictures of the pyramids, one of the great wonders of the ancient world. But things had taken a turn quickly when D'Angelo remarked, "Wow! It's hard to believe those were built by extraterrestrials."

Gran had thought it was a joke, but the more he talked to D'Angelo about it, the more it was clear his grandson believed that nonsense. How could he be so wrong?

"D'Angelo, that's simply not true. You can look it up!"

"Where, Gran, in one of your *sources*?"

"Yes!" Gran stroked the whiskers on his chin thoughtfully.

"Well, I have my *own* sources," said D'Angelo, and he pulled out his newsfeed. Sure enough, multiple articles—at least eight or nine—referenced the pyramids being built by aliens. To Gran, it seemed obviously wrong, but here was D'Angelo's feed, with hundreds of comments from people who agreed it was all true.

"Look, kid. You can't really *believe* this stuff. It's flat hogwash."

D'Angelo was getting annoyed. "Of course *you'd* say that, Gran. You've been brainwashed by the mainstream media. But I've done everything you guys have told me to do online.

- *"Do I have multiple sources? Yes."*
- *"Do they cite authors? Yes."*
- *"Can I find lots of independent sites that say the same thing? Yes."*

"Well, true, but—" Gran tried to comment.

D'Angelo's voice quivered a bit. "Just because *you* don't believe something doesn't make it wrong. Adults make mistakes all the time, but they almost *never* want to admit to them. So, case closed. You're just hypocrites. You only agree when I think what you want me to think. You've got your facts. I've got mine—end of story."

D'Angelo slammed the door so hard Gran's cuckoo clock sounded a sad half-chirp.

Gran stared intently at the closed door, his head cocked to the side. The door itself was no problem. He could think of a thousand ways to get it open if needed. The grandchild, on the other side, was another matter. Had D'Angelo really just slammed the door on him? Were children supposed to do that to their grandparents? Gram and Gran had lived the most rambunctious, rollicking, rambling life imaginable. They'd been everywhere there was to be and seen everything there was to see and then gone back and done it all over again! But somehow, their lives had never had grandchildren in them—until now.

Gran knew that sometimes the best way to solve a problem was to create a different problem and solve that one instead. And as he stared at the chair, it came to him. The problem wasn't D'Angelo's beliefs or his anger. It was too much sitting around. And that just wouldn't do.

The girls are all out, thought Gran, *but what could D'Angelo and I do?*

The boardwalk amusement park! Yes! What ten-year-old boy could resist those bright colors, the joyful sounds, the games, and the prizes? Frozen custard! Cotton candy! Temporary tattoos! The day had started out as a dud, but an amusement park would set it right in no time!

He knocked on the door of the kids' bedroom.

There was no answer.

He put his lips to the door.

"Amusement park," he whispered, but not very quietly.

There was a rustling within.

"Ammmuuuuuuuuuusssemennnnt paarrrrrrrrrkkk," he said, more loudly.

From inside, footsteps came close to the door.

"AAAMMMMMMUUUUUUUSEEMMMENNNT—"

The door flung open.

"Did you say…amusement park?" asked D'Angelo.

* * *

Universe of Diversion was Barnaby's Corner's oldest (and only) amusement park. It sat on the end of the Barnaby Boardwalk inside a giant castle made of concrete. The castle itself was entirely hollow, with no roof, and inside there were colorful booths and small buildings that contained various attractions.

Hollow though it was, the exterior of the Universe of Diversion was magnificent. In each of the stained-glass windows going up the towers and walls of the castle, a different miniature scene was depicted. There was a dashing young man giving a rose to a long-haired princess, a group of red-nosed revelers clinking mugs, and a beautiful unicorn. At the top of the tallest tower, a hulking, mechanical dragon gripped the masonry. The dragon had not one, but seven heads, each staring in a different direction, and if they had not been so goofy looking, with big googly eyes and red tongues lolling out of their mouths, they might have even been a little bit scary.

"Quite a dragon, eh?" Gran asked D'Angelo.

"That's a hydra, Gran, not a dragon."

"Oh?"

"Yeah, see? Seven heads. If you try to cut off one of its heads, two grow back in their place."

"Better not cut them off, then."

"But if you don't cut them off, then they'll eat you!"

"That's quite the pickle," Gran pondered. "Heads a go-go. The more you tangle with it, the more heads it has."

"Heads a what-what?" asked D'Angelo.

"Heads a go-go!" chirped Gran. "Honestly, what is it with you kids not understanding the hip new slang? It means 'aplenty' or 'in abundance.' It means there's a lot of something."

"A go-go," said D'Angelo slowly. "I like that. Don't tell Deja. This one's mine."

Every evening, just after the sun set, the seven heads of the hydra would turn their mechanical mouths to the sky and belch fire in a spectacular display. But now it was close to noon. It was a blazing, cloudless day, and the boardwalk was covered by dozens of people and twice as many seagulls.

As D'Angelo watched, one brave seagull detached from the flock overhead and dove down, snatching a french fry right out of the hand of a large man in a green baseball cap.

"Hey!" the man yelled.

"Bad luck," Gran said to the man sympathetically.

"It ain't luck," the man said, exasperated. "You know how it is. One time, there was one seagull, and someone fed it. So that seagull brought his friends. People fed them, and then before you know it there were a million of 'em, and nobody wanted to feed 'em then, but it was too late. You gotta feed 'em, or they'll just steal what they want. Don't make no difference to them whether you're feeding them on purpose or by accident. Eventually this whole place is gonna be nothing but seagulls."

"Seagulls a go-go," Gran said.

"You said it mister. Seagulls a go-go."

D'Angelo and Gran stepped up to one of the four gates that led into Universe of Diversion. A willowy blonde teenager in a cheap pink princess dress beamed at them from the ticket booth. "Hey y'all," she said in a bright Texas accent, "Welcome to Universe of Diversion. That'll be six bucks." As she spoke, she chewed a sizeable pink chunk of bubblegum.

Gran handed the money to the girl. "Thank you," he said.

They went inside. "Well, D'Angelo, what do you want to do first?" D'Angelo looked around. Many of the attractions were contained within their own booths or buildings, so he couldn't see what they were, but the names were wild and intriguing: THE MYSTERY OF THE FIVE RINGS. THE MUMMY'S TOMB. CAPTAIN TADPOLE'S LIFE-PRESERVER EXTRAVAGANZA. MEGAHAUNTED SUPERHOUSE. PLANET ZABBIX GLORP PARADE.

D'Angelo continued to survey the Universe. There were

a few counters with all kinds of stuffed animals, small plastic toys, glow sticks, and other prizes behind them with their price in tickets prominently displayed. Finally, his eye landed on an open ring toss booth. That, at least, was familiar. It wasn't his favorite, but it was a good place to start.

"I want to do the ring toss," he told Gran.

"Great!" said Gran, "Ring toss is what amusement parks are all about!"

A willowy blonde teenager in a cheap, pink, princess uniform beamed at them from the ring toss booth. Hey y'all," she said in a bright Texas accent. "Welcome to Ring Toss. That'll be fifty cents a ring, or a dollar for three." As she spoke, she chewed a sizeable pink chunk of bubblegum.

"Uhhh…" said D'Angelo, looking back towards the entrance where, sure enough, a different willowy blonde teenager in a cheap pink princess uniform was chewing bubblegum and waiting for visitors. "Do I know you?"

"I git that a lot," the girl said. "My sister, Tammy, runs the ticket booth. So, what'll it be, one toss or three?"

"Three is a better deal," said D'Angelo. "Let's get three. I'll take two tosses, and you can take one. OK, Gran?"

"Sounds good," said Gran as he handed a dollar to the girl. She gave him three red plastic rings.

D'Angelo took his two rings from Gran, placed one on the railing in front of him, and squinted. In front of him, there was an array of glass bottles. Most of them were green, but three in the back were yellow, and one was bright red. He had read about Ring Toss. It wasn't exactly a scam, but it was set up for people to lose. For the ring to settle on the bottleneck, it had to fall almost straight down from above. If it was at even a little angle, it would bounce off.

But he had also read how to fix that. If he spun the ring sideways like a frisbee when he threw it, it wouldn't wobble. If he threw it in a big arc, it would fall almost straight down. If he did both those things, he could win. He decided to play it safe and aim for one of the close green bottles.

Taking the ring between his thumb and forefinger, he took a deep breath, then tossed the ring lightly into the air in a large lazy arc. It landed between two of the bottles, clattered for a moment, and fell to the floor.

He sighed and grabbed the second ring off the railing. He snapped his wrist hard as he launched it higher in the air than the first. It went up, up, up, and then it came down almost exactly on the neck of one of the green bottles. *Almost, but not quite,* he thought.

"Bad luck, sport," said Gran.

"It's not luck," D said. "It's skill. I just have to practice."

"Sure," said Gran, "just like playing the piano. But once you practice playing the piano, you'll know how to play any song you want. After practicing Ring Toss, you'll…know how to win Ring Toss." He smiled a little wistfully. "Not that I'm one to talk." Then he tossed his ring with an expert snap of the wrist. It went up, spinning fast, and then fell right onto the neck of the red bottle.

"Five hundred tickets!" the girl cheered.

"How'd you learn to do that, Gran?" asked D'Angelo.

"I like amusement parks," Gran said matter-of-factly. "You want to pick a different place?"

D'Angelo thought for a moment. "The Mummy's Tomb!" he said. "That sounds cool. I wonder what kind of ride it is."

Gran looked at D'Angelo, confused, but D'Angelo didn't notice because he was already on his way across the Universe of Diversion.

The Mummy's Tomb was a giant pyramid with a large emerald eye at the top. A few intrepid kids were climbing all the way up to the top and then sliding down, shrieking with joy.

"Think this one was made by aliens too?" said Gran with a wink.

D'Angelo rolled his eyes. "I don't know, but if every source I found said that it was, I wouldn't believe *you* instead." He walked off in a huff.

Whoops, Gran thought, regretting his joke. He hadn't realized how sore D'Angelo still was about the whole pyramids thing.

The door was rather low, and even D'Angelo had to duck a little as they went in, traveling down a long, dark, narrow corridor of stone towards an eerie, green light coming from a large chamber at the end. They entered.

A willowy blonde teenager in a cheap, pink, Egyptian uniform beamed at them from the chamber. "Hey y'all," she said in a bright Texas accent. "Welcome to The Mummy's Tomb. That'll be fifty cents a ring, or a dollar for three." As she spoke, she chewed a sizeable pink chunk of bubblegum.

In front of her was an array of small sarcophagi, standing up. Most of them were green, but three were yellow, and one was red.

"Is this..." D'Angelo began. "Is this a ring toss?"

"Naw, silly," the girl said. "This is the Mummy's Tomb, y'all!"

"What do we do in the Mummy's Tomb?" he asked.

"You take these here rings," the girl said, pointing to a pile of red plastic rings. "Then you toss 'em in the air and try to get 'em over a Mummy's head."

"So, it's Ring Toss."

The girl giggled nervously as if he had told a joke that wasn't very funny. "It's the muh-meee's tooo-emb," she continued, stretching out the words as if he were a little kid.

D'Angelo tried a different tactic. "Are you Tammy?" he asked the girl.

"Oh no. That's my sister," she said. "I'm Sammy. We're the Funnel sisters. From Algo, Texas. Every summer we pick up an' move out here to get jobs at the Universe of Diversion. We git away from that dry West Texas heat and enjoy this-here fresh ocean breeze. We rent a big ol' house down at the end of the boardwalk, live family style, and grill out every night. We work cheap and live large."

"Do your names all end in -ammy?"

"Goodness no. Sammy's not even my name. It's just a nickname."

"It's short for Samantha, right?"

"Naw, silly. It's short for Sandwich."

"Your name is Sandwich?"

"Yes indeed. Why ya lookin' at me like that? Sandwich is an ol' family name. What's your name?"

"D'Angelo."

"And what's that short for?"

"It's not short for anything. It's just D'Angelo."

"What's a D'Angelo?"

"A D'Angelo isn't anything. It's just a name."

"At least a sandwich is *something*," Sammy said haughtily.

D'Angelo could see this wasn't going to go anywhere. "Gran, I wanna try something else."

"What's up? Too scared of the Mummy's Curse?" asked Gran. He winced. His jokes hadn't been landing today. Why did he feel the need to try another one?

"No. It's just that I want to do something else."

"Something else? You want to leave the the park?"

"No, I just want to do something else."

This time, D'Angelo did see Gran's confused look.

"You know, like a ride? Tilt-a-Whirl? Bumper cars? Maybe Skee-Ball?"

Gran looked at D'Angelo blankly. "But this is an amusement park."

"Right, so where's the rides?"

"You there," said Gran, "Sandwich. What kinds of amusements do they have in an amusement park?"

The girl chuckled. "Why, that's an easy one. Ring Toss!"

"Yeah," said D'Angelo, "but what else?"

Blank stares greeted him.

D'Angelo shook his head vigorously. "No," he said, "look…" He pulled out his phone and typed "AMUSEMENT PARK" into the search bar, then selected images. "See?" On his phone, images of bumper cars, merry-go-rounds, Ferris wheels, log flumes, drop towers, tests of strength, and a dozen other attractions appeared as he scrolled.

"But those aren't ring tosses!" Gran exclaimed.

"Yeah, but look here, Gran. They've got all kinds of stuff in amusement parks. You ever been to Coney Island?" Because they lived in Brooklyn, D'Angelo's family had been to the Coney Island boardwalk dozens of times. Each of the kids had their favorite rides at Luna Park, the amusement park on the boardwalk. Nia liked the Cyclone because it was an old-time classic, a wooden rollercoaster that had been in operation for at least a century. Deja, predictably, liked the carousel for its pretty horses and mild thrills. And D'Angelo, though he would NEVER EVER IN A MILLION YEARS ADMIT IT, loved the Tea Party Teacups more than anything.

He loved the way they spun and danced dizzily, sloshing him this way and that.

Sammy had taken an interest in the conversation. "Whaddya mean? They got stuff that ain't ring tosses in those there amusement parks?"

"YES!" D'Angelo shouted.

Sammy and Gran looked at each other in bewilderment. "Sounds fake," said Gran. "Sad!" shouted Sammy.

"C'mon, Gran," said D'Angelo dejectedly. "Let's go home. I'm tired of Ring Toss."

Gran's face fell. "Are you sure?" he asked. "Don't you want to try something else? How about Captain Tadpole's Life-Preserver Extravaganza?"

"Is it just Ring Toss?"

"Well…"

"I want. To go. Home."

* * *

Walking in circles around the Great Thinking Chair, Gran shuddered at his memory of recent events. A glow-in-the-dark mini-frisbee bought with his 500 Universe Tickets, and a chocolate frozen custard and fries, bought with regular money, had brightened D'Angelo's mood and saved the day from utter disaster, but Gran was tired. For the first time, he was "feeling his age," and he didn't like it one bit. Finally, he stopped his pacing and took the unusual step of actually sitting down.

"How was I supposed to know?" he grumbled. "Doesn't everybody love Ring Toss? It's the only thing amusement parks have!" He tried to remember other parks he'd been to, but it was like the Universe of Diversion was the only thing he could recall.

Like much of the furniture in the Tower, the Great Thinking Chair had been there when Gran and Gram moved in. It was a mechanical marvel. Tastefully concealed in its arms were levers and switches that would raise it, lower it, increase or decrease its lumbar support and recline the back. But the most marvelous lever was one Gran had discovered by accident. It didn't make the chair more comfortable.

It made the Thinking Chair sink below the floor on a pedestal. One foot. Five feet. Ten feet. It came to rest in a huge room full of rows and rows of tall glass cases connected by cords and wires, all faintly humming and beeping and blipping. To Gran, the air smelled like brand-new numbers. He didn't know what "brand-new numbers" meant, but he knew that's how it smelled.

He was in the Tower's computer room.

"Computer," Gran said to the room, "Find me: Universe of Diversion, history of."

* * *

As it turned out, there had been a documentary made several years ago about the Universe of Diversion. Gran settled into the Great Thinking Chair and watched it half distracted, waiting for something to catch his eye. As was his usual habit, he had turned the sound off and was using the subtitles to follow along. He didn't know exactly why he always did it that way, but he guessed that after so many years reading books, it was the only way his brain felt comfortable.

As he watched, the other half of his mind turned around and around, throwing off questions like a generator throws off bolts of electricity. He had been all sorts of places, so why had he gotten so confused about amusement parks? And he had known all kinds of people, so why was he so confused about how to talk to his grandson? And why did D'Angelo see conspiracies everywhere he looked? And how could he teach the boy that some sources could be trusted and some sources couldn't?

And why had he and Gram been strangers from their grandchildren for so many years? It had all seemed to make some kind of sense at the time. He and Gram had thought they were seeing the whole world, but they were only seeing a part of it, and they had been missing the most important part of all.

The story of Universe of Diversion flickered on the screen. When it was built, it had been called Babel Castle instead. There was an old TV news report from the 60s showing Barnaby Babel himself cutting the ribbon for its opening. But then Babel had disappeared, and the rumors began. Some said he had entered the Haunted House ride and then never left—that his ghost now haunted the Castle. That surprised Gran. *What Haunted House ride?* he thought. People started to stay away from the place. The rides broke down from disuse. The hydra-heads stopped breathing their fire every night, Babel Castle went bankrupt, and the park was set to be knocked down.

But then, at the last moment, a group of wealthy investors known as Universe Capital bought the castle. They changed the name to Universe of Diversion and came up with a simple, ambitious plan. Gran sat up and turned his full attention to the subtitles. This part looked like it might be interesting.

INTERVIEWER: Tell us about your plan.

MAN IN A SUIT: It was simple. When we reopened Universe of Diversion, we had all kinds of attractions, just like Babel Castle had.

The screen displayed images of that first year. Gran could see a Ferris wheel, a dunk tank, and a lazy river ride.

MAN IN A SUIT: But at the end of that year, we built a computer program — an algorithm — to analyze our rides and give people more of what they wanted. Our goal was to maximize profit.

INTERVIEWER: You wanted to make as much

money as possible.

MAN IN A SUIT: Yes, and as fast as possible. We had the algorithm analyze our records and found that our number one moneymaker was Ring Toss.

INTERVIEWER: Why was that?

MAN IN A SUIT: (shrugging) No idea. The computer didn't know, and we didn't care. The point was...it made the most money. And the algorithm – the computer program – told us we should build more because that's what the people liked. So the next year, we tripled the ring toss booths.

INTERVIEWER: And made triple the money?

MAN IN A SUIT: Not exactly. It turned out that when people saw three identical Ring Toss booths, they said, "Hey, what happened to the other rides?"

INTERVIEWER: So you got rid of the Ring Toss booths?

MAN IN A SUIT: Of course not! We spent good money on those booths. No. The algorithm said to build even *more*. That way, people wouldn't even remember there were other rides out there.

INTERVIEWER: So they only saw the same thing over and over?

MAN IN A SUIT: Yeah. The algorithm gave them fun names, like FIVE CLOWNS IN A KANGAROO'S POUCH, but it just kept recommending more Ring Toss. After a while, people just figured Ring Toss was the only game in town. After a while, it WAS the only game in town.

INTERVIEWER: But that's not what people want at all! You were tricking them.

MAN IN A SUIT: (waving hand casually) Trickery schmickery! They liked it, so the algorithm just kept saying to give them what they wanted.

INTERVIEWER: But surely people complained? I mean, they didn't want *only* one game. You had to know that.

MAN IN A SUIT: That's the great part! After a while, people stopped thinking about the old rides. Even when visitors who'd seen other parks started asking questions, other attendees just told them they were victims of the "fake amusements" that the Mainstream Amusement Park Establishment wanted them to accept. The only thing that people in Barnaby's Corner saw was the Ring Toss booths, so it was the only thing they thought belonged in a park. Here's a little secret: if you keep telling people the same thing over and over, sooner or later, they'll stop fighting you. In fact, they'll fight with anyone who says you're wrong.

INTERVIEWER: Did it work?

MAN IN A SUIT: Look around you. You tell me. Why brainwash people when they'll just do it to themselves?

INTERVIEWER: You're a monster.

MAN IN A SUIT: I'm a businessman. And all I did was buy an algorithm to give the people what they wanted. Since when was making people happy a crime?

Gran leaned back in the Great Thinking Chair, stunned. "Ring Toss a go-go," he murmured to himself. Universe of Diversion was run by a computer program, and he'd been fooled like everyone else in Barnaby's Corner.

But now he thought he had an idea about how to help his grandson break out of his pyramids conspiracy theories. After all, it was an algorithm that was running D'Angelo's newsfeed, too.

Can you help Gran convince D'Angelo to reconsider what he's learning from his newsfeed?
Turn the page for some hints from Gran.

Hint from Gran

This is a tricky one! There's no secret clue or aha moment that will give you the answer. Just like in the real world, the best we can do is make some strong arguments and keep an open mind. But consider the UNIVERSE OF DIVERSION. Why do the residents of Barnaby's Corner think Ring Toss is the only amusement park game? Why don't they trust the people who have seen other parks in real life? Even if people liked Ring Toss at first, would a park that *only* offered one game be a good time?

Now, let's think about D'Angelo's newsfeed. People get exposed to **newsfeed bias** when their feeds keep serving them the same types of biased information and they aren't exposed to other views. I tend to rely on mainstream media for a larger portion of what I know, though I look at other sources, too. Consider:

1. What makes "**mainstream**" media mainstream? How did they earn that title, and does that give them any more **credibility** than, say, a random blog post? (Do mainstream media—like big newspapers—have an incentive to get things right?)
2. Is there a way to check on things that both the mainstream media and D'Angelo's sources say? Can I help show one source is more trustworthy than another?

3. D'Angelo has been getting his news from social media, which means the stories he reads have been chosen for him by an **algorithm**—a computer program that chooses what he sees. But a lot of social media algorithms aren't really meant to give you an honest picture of the world. They're meant to show you things you find interesting or will get emotional about—that's what media companies call **engagement**. And because engagement is what makes money, algorithms will recommend anything that keeps people engaged. It's just like the amusement park. They keep recommending the same thing until that's all you get. The algorithm knows D'Angelo likes reading about aliens building the pyramids and will read lots of articles on this, so what might it be doing?

D'Angelo is right that we need to keep an open mind about the world and stay **skeptical** about sources of information. So how can I be confident that I'm getting better information than D'Angelo?

Conclusion: The Conspiracy Behind the Conspiracies

"D'Angelo, come on over to my study," called Gran. "I'd like to apologize."

It took D'Angelo a good ten minutes to make his way across the thirty feet that separated his room and where Gran was, but he edged in, half unsure whether he'd really be getting an apology or if the fight would continue.

Gran took a deep breath. "Buddy, I'm sorry. I'm sorry about the Universe of Diversion. And I'm sorry about our fight this morning too. About the pyramids. You made some good points." Gran stood up from his Great Thinking Chair. "And I was thinking about Ring Toss."

D'Angelo groaned. "Not Ring Toss again! I think I'm just about Ring Tossed out!"

Gran nodded. "I know, I know, but thinking about it is how I figured out you were right, and I just wanted to think about this topic with you—as philosophers in training if you will." Gran knew D'Angelo wouldn't be able to resist a philosophical conversation. The other day, D'Angelo had said that he'd like to study philosophy in college since, as he understood it, being a philosopher meant thinking all day and then telling other people that everything they knew was wrong.

D'Angelo hesitated.

"Please," Gran said, motioning to his Great Thinking

Chair. "Take a seat."

D'Angelo sat. Gran continued. "I was thinking about Ring Toss. I was thinking about how the Universe of Diversion got so Ring Tossed up."

D'Angelo smiled. "It was Ring Toss a go-go in there."

If there's only one victory today, thought Gran, *it's that D'Angelo now likes calling things "a go-go."*

"You said it," responded Gran. "How'd that happen? You think anyone likes Ring Toss so much they'd want a castle full of it?"

D'Angelo shook his head and pondered. "Maybe," he said. "Maybe everyone tells them they need to quit it with the Ring Toss booths, but they don't care. They can't get enough Ring Toss booths, and that's that. That's how it is," he scowled. "Whoever's at the top calls the shots, and everyone else just has to take what they're given."

"Nice reasoning," said Gran. "So it seems like the real question would be: who's at the top, and how do they think?"

"I guess so."

Gran moved closer to the Great Thinking Chair. "I think I know who's on top. The big cheese. The kahuna grande. I want to show you something. Pull that lever there," he said. It was the lever that brought the Thinking Chair to the computer room.

* * *

After they had watched the documentary on Universe of

Diversion, Gran said, "So there you have it."

"Universe Capital is on top. They're calling the shots," said D'Angelo, after blasting Gran with about 1,000 questions on how he possibly had a secret computer room he'd been keeping from him.

"Well…" Gran scratched his chin, "Yes, and no. I mean, don't get me wrong, they're the ones responsible, but they did something here. They set up some rules, and then they let the *rules* call the shots."

"What do you mean?"

"Well, they made a rule to tell them what to do. Whichever booth made the most money, they'd keep opening more like it. And because they made more of that booth, those booths made the most money. Universe Capital didn't care *which* booth made the most money. They didn't even know. But they had a set of rules to follow. An algorithm."

"Universe Capital chose the algorithm," said D'Angelo. "The algorithm chose the rides."

"Exactly." Gran agreed.

"Neat setup. If anyone complained, they could say, "We didn't make the choices. The algorithm did!'"

"Sounds like a conspiracy to me. An invisible hand manipulating the results."

"It does to me too, Gran. I'm glad you're beginning to see how many conspiracies there are."

Gran felt a little queasy. He knew the next thing he said

would be crucial.

"So, I think it's *possible* you might be a victim of an accidental conspiracy."

"What?"

"I was thinking about the aliens-built-the-pyramids thing…" Gran began.

D'Angelo's anger returned. "Maybe your generation just doesn't get it. Besides, I read this *all the time*. So it can't be wrong. I showed you my newsfeed earlier."

"You did."

"So?"

"Well, it's like how the park turned into Ring Toss city. Things like social media are controlled by algorithms that try to guess what you want to read. The programs aren't evil, but they don't really care about whether they are sharing good stories or bad ones. If you're looking for a secret force that's trying to tell you what to read and think, that's exactly what this is!"

"Wait, what?" D'Angelo shifted in his chair. He wasn't sure where Gran was going, but conspiracy theories were the main thing he liked to read about, and this was one he hadn't heard of.

"Well, the algorithm looks at what you read and how much time you spend reading it. It looks at the topics you respond to or even get emotional about. So, when you started reading about aliens, the algorithm figured out you were interested in them and showed you a whole bunch of stories about them. Over and over and over. The algorithm isn't necessarily trying to trick you. It's trying to make you happy because it wants you to stay online! But if you only read what it shares with you, you'll just hear the same things repeatedly."

D'Angelo was quiet for a moment. "So my newsfeed ends up all aliens."

"You said it. Aliens a go-go."

There was a long pause. Gran and D'Angelo stared at the chair for a good long while. Finally, in the softest voice, Gran broke the silence.

"It's not right for me to tell you what to believe. There's definitely a possibility that aliens built the pyramids. But I try to avoid newsfeed bias by seeking out lots of reputable sources beyond what some algorithm feeds me. And when I look at those reputable sources—encyclopedias and historians and archaeologists and, yes, mainstream media too—they say that's not true," Gran said.

"Oh," said D'Angelo, his face lightin up. "It's kind of like cherry picking – but supersized! But how do you know you can trust the U.S. media? Isn't it possible *they* have a bias, like rooting for the home team?"

"By gum, D'Angelo! That's a fantastic point! I'd never thought about it that way. There are tons of great, reputable sources all over the planet. Anywhere the press is free, you'll find them."

"OK, good. I get nervous only trusting one perspective, especially if it's the one everyone takes for granted."

"Exactly. And, D?" Until this moment, Gran always had called D'Angelo by his full name, never using the nickname his siblings gave him. His voice grew soft again. "I know this is cheesy, but no matter what you believe, I'll always love you. I just want to be sure it's what *you* believe, not what some algorithm fooled you into thinking."

Another pause.

"Gran, the internet can be a confusing place."

"It certainly can be a universe of diversion. That's why I have my Great Thinking Chair. Sometimes I need to reason things out."

"Gran?"

"Yes, D?"

"Would you mind if I sat in the chair for a while?"

"I think that'd be just fine," said Gran.

Chapter 10: Pure Puffery

There were few things Nia, D'Angelo, and Deja enjoyed more than a friendly sibling argument. And whenever the children couldn't find anything else to argue about, they could always argue about Gram and Gran's wild stories.

Today's debate had started over a map which hung on the wall in their bedroom. The room Gram and Gran had given them for the summer was obviously not supposed to be for children. The far wall was nothing but floor-to-ceiling windows looking out of the Tower. The view was spectacular but a little alarming. D'Angelo had loved it at once, and Nia had soon gotten over her initial butterflies and found the view intriguing. But Deja stayed as far away as she could. She insisted on taking the bed farthest from the windows. She couldn't exactly explain it, but being so high up made her feel weird, like the whole world was a dream and she could wake up at any moment. The rooftop, where the chickens lived, felt different. There was a fence to keep her safe and cute chickens to keep her distracted. But the windows here showed *everything*, and she couldn't help but imagine one just popping out if she pressed it too hard.

"It's totally safe, Day," Nia had explained. "Barnaby Babel hired the best architects and scientists in the world. It's like flying in a plane. It doesn't seem like it should stay up, but science says it should, so it does."

"But I've never been in a plane! I don't know what they're like!" said Deja.

"Oh. Right. Well, trust me. That's how they work."

Deja had not found her sister's explanation convincing. She continued to act like the windows could suck her out at any moment.

To keep her mind from the thousand feet of clear air just outside of their bedroom, Deja had spent a lot of time inspecting the other three walls. Fortunately for her, they were fascinating. The room had likely been a library of some kind before Gram and Gran made it ready for their visitors. There were tall shelves everywhere. Some had books on them: fiction, nonfiction, and even a healthy collection of old-timey comic books, which both Deja and D'Angelo loved.

Other shelves bore objects: photographs, fossils, geodes, small stone statues, brightly colored feathers, strange brass instruments, egg timers of various sizes filled with sand or mysterious liquids, three-dimensional puzzles made of wood and metal, a clear plastic maze with a little blob of mercury in it. Every time she looked, she found something new. And the walls were no different. On the wall above the beds, there were paintings, tapestries, and framed maps.

This time, Deja had noticed a map of Atlantis. When she pointed it out, Nia told her Atlantis wasn't real. Then, D'Angelo told her that Atlantis was a myth, but that it was based on a real island that had once existed. Nia said D'Angelo didn't know what he was talking about. D'Angelo countered that if Atlantis didn't exist, how come there were so many different stories about it?

That had gotten them started about Gram and Gran's stories.

"I hope they're true," said Deja. "That would be so cool!"

Nia sighed. "I think Gram and Gran are the kind of people who like to joke around. Telling stories is just the way they have fun with each other. They're, like, a million years old. They've got to do *something* to keep things lively."

"See?" cried Deja. "A million years old!"

"It's just a figure of speech, Day. I meant they're super old."

Deja looked a little hurt, as if Nia had been trying to trick her. "So we can't trust them?" she asked.

Nia thought about it. "I don't know. I think there's… like…different *kinds* of trust? Like, I would trust you to keep a secret about who I have a crush on—"

"Mike Lopez," her siblings said in chorus.

Nia blushed, but continued, "But I wouldn't trust you to drive me to the hospital. Even if you promised to be careful. Because—"

Before she could finish her train of thought, an electronic chime rang out in the penthouse. After a moment, they heard Gram's muffled voice exclaiming something, and then Gran's joined in.

"The doorbell! I want to see who it is!" said Deja. She ran out with the other two following behind.

When they arrived at the door, they saw quite a sight. Ruthbert Rugglesford was standing in the hallway, looking less buoyant than usual with a hangdog expression on his face. He held his purple top hat in his hands and was squeezing it in anxiety.

"Now Gram…" Ruthbert was saying.

"Don't 'now Gram' me!" Gram snapped. "Every time we've let you around the kids, they've ended up doing something awful sneaky."

"Or criminal!" Gran added.

Gram continued, "And now you come back here with another one of your nutty schemes."

"But Gram," Ruthbert protested. "I promise you, there's no scheme—no scheme at all! I feel ever so badly about what happened. I'm trying to make it up to you—to all of you—with a one-of-a-kind, once-in-a-lifetime experience, and—"

"I bet you've got an angle," Gran sputtered. "I bet you've got a million of 'em! What's your angle, you…you…*angler*?"

A tear rolled down Ruthbert's cheek. He straightened himself up and tilted his head back in a dignified manner.

"I swear," he said, "on my honor as a Rugglesford. My only wish is to make up for any…err…misunderstandings we may have had. I suppose I'm not very good around kids, having had none of my own. I just don't know what to do with them. But unless I'm very much mistaken, this is something they would really enjoy—a hot-air balloon ride!"

"I don't know, Ruthbert," said Gram.

"I understand completely," Ruthbert responded. "You must be wondering if it's safe. Well, let me tell you, this balloon is a marvel!" He reached behind his back and pulled a large, colorful brochure from what Nia hoped was his pocket instead of his pants.

Ruthbert flapped the brochure grandly in the air. "This balloon is the top of the line!" He opened the brochure to a page that showed a large candy-colored hot air balloon on it. Sure enough, the words TOP OF THE LINE were printed next to the picture. "It's virtually indestructible!" He flipped to another page which showed a group of smiling passengers in the basket of the balloon. The caption underneath said, VIRTUALLY INDESTRUCTIBLE! "It's made of space-age polymers manufactured by the most brilliant scientists in the universe!" The page he showed them depicted two scientists in lab coats. Sure enough, the words on the page were SPACE-AGE POLYMERS MADE BY WORLD-CLASS SCIENTISTS! "It's the world's safest hot-air balloon!" On this page, the balloon was soaring through a clear blue sky.

Beneath it there was a medal that said, WORLD'S SAFEST BALLOON. "And it has FIVE—count 'em—FIVE brand new never-fail safety features," he finished, showing them a page that listed FIVE NEW NEV-R-FAIL® SAFETY FEATURES.

"A hot-air balloon ride does sound pretty neat...," said Nia.

Ruthbert looked delighted by her agreement. "My girl, it's not just *any* balloon ride! It's a ride on an unparalleled wonder of modern technology, the most magnificent, exhilarating balloon in the history of the world! Just imagine wafting into the warm and welcoming ether in a craft of unsurpassed safety and sophistication! Picture looking down at Barnaby's Corner while a balmy zephyr zooms you over the sights!"

Deja's stomach lurched at the words "looking down."

"Um, Mr. Ruthbert?" she said, "How high up does the balloon go?"

Ruthbert seemed delighted to answer the question. "About 3,000 feet. Almost three times as high as the Tower! Now *that's* a view." He spread his arms wide and gave his top hat a little razzle-dazzle shake.

"You said the kids are only here for another week, right? Time is short! Let's show them this place in *style*."

* * *

Two days later, Ruthbert sent a text to Gran before dawn:

WEATHER GOOD ☀ LIGHT BREEZE 🎈 🦒

"Balloon giraffe?" Gran mumbled to himself as he lay in bed in the dark. "Well, it has been some time since I looked a giraffe right in the eye. Just like the old days."

A moment later, a second text came through:

PHINEAS WILL BE THERE AT 6AM

By six, everyone was up and ready to go, although none too awake. They stood outside of the Tower, Gram and Gran sipping coffee from thermoses. Phineas pulled up in a large twelve-seater van, and they climbed in.

"Everyone feeling frisky?" Phineas asked with a smile. "I've been up since 3 a.m. helping Ruthbert get the balloon ready." He, too, was drinking coffee from a thermos. He started the van and began driving them north, out of town, on a road that led into deep woods.

As he drove, he explained the day's plans. "I'll take you to the launch site, then I'll drive to the landing site and wait for you. Once you land, we'll pack the balloon up and head home from there. You'll be taking off from the northwest of the island, near a place called Barnaby's Folly. That's where Barnaby Babel started building another tower before he disappeared. The building didn't get too far, but he cleared a lot of land, so it's a nice spot to take off from."

"Phineas, do you really, um, *trust* Ruthbert?" asked Nia.

"Haven't spent much time with him before today," he

said. "I'm strictly here as the island's aviation coordinator and taxi driver. But he *does* have a license. I checked that out for you."

The trees started getting thinner and thinner, and then they were driving in a huge open field that sloped gently down to a placid sea. They could see the balloon, a little ball—covered in pink, purple, red, and white—at first. It got bigger and bigger. Then they saw a large, top-hatted figure standing next to it. Phineas pulled up to the balloon, and they got out. "I'll stick around to see you've launched safely, and I'll pick you up in a few hours," he said as the kids marched toward Ruthbert.

Ruthbert beckoned them proudly towards the balloon. His top hat was tied under his chin by a strip of purple felt, and he was wearing bright green goggles and a heavy leather coat, underneath which he wore his typical array of button-down shirts. As they got closer, Deja realized that the goggles weren't aviator's goggles, but swim goggles.

Until that moment, Deja had been completely calm. Something inside her just couldn't believe she was *actually* going to get in a rickety wicker basket hanging below a balloon filled by hot air from an open flame—and then soar *thousands* of feet into the sky.

But now the fear hit her all at once. She felt like she was being flipped upside-down, like her legs were up in the air and if she tried to move, she'd float away instead.

She must have looked how she felt, because Ruthbert came over to her and knelt, so he was almost at eye level with her. "Feeling a little jittery, eh?" he asked kindly. "Well let's see what I can do to put your mind at ease. First, you should know that I am a licensed private balloon pilot." He opened his wallet and unfolded a certificate from inside it. UNITED STATES OF AMERICA DEPARTMENT OF TRANSPORTATION FEDERAL AVIATION ADMINISTRATION, it read. PRIVATE PILOT. "I guess I'm no astronaut," he whispered wistfully, "but this was the closest I could get."

Deja had to admit, it did make her feel a bit better. Ruthbert usually seemed so full of…well…hot air, but that license looked completely legit.

Ruthbert continued. "Second, I'll let you hold on to this." He produced the same brochure that he had shown them the other day.

"It's got detailed descriptions of the balloon's five special safety features. If you start to get scared, take a gander at them. You'll see how safe you really are." He handed the brochure to her. Deja gripped it tightly.

Then Ruthbert stood back up. "Are we ready to go?" he asked. He swung a door in the basket open. Inside, there were six back-to-back chairs with shoulder straps on them. Deja had been imagining that they would be standing in the basket, but the chairs made her feel more secure. She was no longer terrified, but she was still extremely nervous.

"Gram," she whispered.

Gram looked down at her.

"What is it, honey?"

"I'm scared. I'm not sure I can do this."

Gram nodded. "You know you don't have to if you don't want to. You and I can just stay here on the ground, and I'll call Phineas to pick us up. Gran and I didn't get this old by ignoring our fear."

For a moment, Deja seriously considered turning back, but as she watched her siblings climb happily into the basket and strap themselves in, she knew she wanted to take the ride.

"It's OK, Gram. I want to do it."

Gram squeezed her shoulder. "Good for you, honey. Gran and I didn't get this old by only listening to our fear, either. Tell you what, you sit right next to me." Deja smiled. She liked that idea.

They walked over to the balloon, and with a gentlemanly flourish, Ruthbert took Deja's hand and guided her into the basket. "That seat in the middle there," he told her. "Gram can be on that side of you, and I'll be on the other, when I take a break from piloting the balloon. Best seat in the house."

Finally, they were settled. "Everybody OK?" asked Ruthbert. "No need for a last-minute bathroom break? Everybody dressed warmly? Remember, it'll get colder the higher up we go."

"I got my long johns on!" Gran shouted happily. "Wouldn't leave home without them!"

Ruthbert pulled on a handle near the balloon's burner and it sprung to life, releasing a thick orange flame that began to fill the balloon with more hot air. It made a tremendous whooshing sound, so loud that Deja couldn't even hear herself think. It was quite soothing in its own way. Deja wasn't sure she wanted to think right at that moment.

The balloon began to rise, pulling at the ropes that had anchored it to the ground. Beneath them, Phineas moved methodically to each of the ropes, untying them from the weights that had made sure the balloon wouldn't drift off until it was time to go. He untied the last one, and now they were truly floating free.

"All right then!" Ruthbert waved out of the basket at Phineas. "Thanks, Phineas. See you at the landing site!"

"Goodbye everyone!" Phineas shouted back. "Have a wonderful time!"

The balloon went up, up, up. It was a curious sensation. To Deja's body, it felt like they were hardly moving. But her eyes could see the ground dwindling beneath them. She could see the waves breaking against the rocks on the desolate north shore of the island, the sea crinkling like a piece of gray-blue paper, and then the endless sheet of the whole Atlantic Ocean seeming to smooth out as they got higher and it became harder to spot the waves. Above her head, she could see the inside of the balloon glow pink, purple, red, and white from the sun.

Ruthbert was checking some instruments on the side of the basket. Apparently satisfied, he nodded his head and released the handle. The flame stopped.

"Ladies and gentlemen," he said, "we are now at cruising altitude. In a moment, I will point out some of the sights to you. But first, let's take a few minutes to appreciate one of my favorite aspects of this noble mode of travel, the silence."

When he stopped talking, Deja could hear what he meant. The silence was remarkable. It was quiet, so quiet that she could hear her family breathing, could hear D'Angelo shifting slightly in his seat.

She squeezed Gram's hand and whispered her name as quietly as she could.

"What is it, Deja?" she whispered back.

"I'm so full of feelings. I don't know if I'm scared or excited."

Gram nodded seriously. "Excitement and fear often feel very similar. It's not how you feel. It's how you act that tells your brain which it is. So tell me. If you *were* excited, how would you act?"

Deja thought for a moment. "I guess I'd yell, 'Wahoo!'" she whispered back.

"Then do it," Gram whispered emphatically.

"But it's so quiet."

"Go for it, sister. Let it blow. Be so loud they'll hear it on the ground!"

Deja took a deep breath.

"WAHOO!" she yelled at the top of her lungs. "WAAAAAHOOOOOOOOOOO!"

For a moment, her yell was swallowed up by the air around them, but then D'Angelo joined in. "OH YEAHHHHH! THAT'S RIGHT! BALLOOOOOOOOOON!"

"AAAAaaaaAAAAaaAAAAA!!" screamed Nia. "AAAAAAAAAAAAAAAAAAAAAAAA!"

"WOOOOOOOOOOOOO!" hooted Gram.

"ALL RIGHT! ALL RIGHT! ALL RIGHT!" went Gran.

"SPLENDID! MAGNIFICENT! OUTSTANDING!" Ruthbert rejoiced.

They laughed until tears ran down their faces.

"Now that we're physically and emotionally acclimated," Ruthbert said, "I would like to draw your attention to the south," he pointed out of the balloon, "where you can see the entirety of Barnaby's Corner, Tower and all!"

Sure enough, the whole town spread out before them like a map, from the docks in the west to the boardwalk on the eastern shore—and right in the middle, the Tower, cutting an imposing figure above it all. Deja almost fancied she could see the rooftop chickens, but at their height and distance, she couldn't be sure if it was a trick of her imagination.

"The unique geography of this island makes it the perfect place for Barnaby Babel to have built that tower, which as you know is strong enough to control the entire internet! And to the north—" Ruthbert said grandly. But Deja never discovered what was to the north, because at that very moment there was a loud SPROING and the basket of the balloon lurched sickeningly and tilted down at an angle, throwing Ruthbert to the floor and causing the passengers to grab onto their seat-straps in terror.

Everything was quiet.

"Nothing to worry about. Everything is in order," said Ruthbert, standing up and steadying himself against the basket's sides. "I'm just going to—"

But Deja never found out what he was going to do, because at that moment there was another SPROING! and the basket lurched again.

"Ruthbert!" cried Gram, pointing up. "The ropes! The ropes connecting us to the balloon!"

Deja looked to where he was pointing. The basket was connected to the balloon by eight thick ropes. Or at least it *had* been connected by eight ropes. But now two of them were trailing off the sides of the basket, completely severed from the balloon that held them aloft.

"I thought you said this balloon was indestructible!" Gran yelled. "It's destructing right before our eyes! You lied again, you criminal! You promised us no more crimes!"

Despite the danger of their situation, Ruthbert seemed more upset by the accusation than the imminent disaster.

"I did NOT break my promise!" he roared. "I looked it up. Puffery is not against the law."

"Puff–what?" screamed Nia.

"Puffery! It's perfectly legal to say something untrue if no reasonable person would believe it. OF COURSE a balloon is destructible! What kind of maniac would think it's not? If I told you I was the greatest dancer in the history of the universe, would you believe me?"

"Not anymore, I wouldn't!" said Deja.

"What would that even mean?" asked Ruthbert. "Greatest how? And who decides? If a lie is so big it's obvious, then you're allowed to say it. Companies do it all the time. The claims just have to be very general…nothing too specific. You know, like 'world's best cup of coffee!'"

"But why—" D'Angelo yelled, "why would you say it then—if everybody is supposed to know it's a lie?"

"That's advertising, baby! And it's more fun that way. Would you rather take a balloon ride, or THE MOST ENJOYABLE BALLOON RIDE OF ALL TIME? Don't you feel safer in a balloon made of SPACE-AGE TECHNOLOGY?"

"I would feel safer in a balloon that wasn't falling apart!" shouted D'Angelo.

Ruthbert nodded solemnly, as if he found this argument persuasive. "I see—"

SPROING!

A third line snapped.

"Take this balloon down, Ruthbert! We're gonna crash!" yelled Gran.

"I don't think we'll make it in time!" Ruthbert said. "But I'll do my best." He walked up the sloping basket and began pulling ropes and pushing buttons.

Even though the basket was now leaning distinctly to one side, Gram unstrapped herself from her seat. "Gran!" she cried. "We've got to buy Ruthbert some time. Remember the English Channel? 1785?"

"Of course, my darling! You're absolutely right!" Gran stood up as well. "But how are we going to tie them together? We don't have any extra rope. Ruthbert, do we have any extra rope?"

"This balloon is equipped with the very best of everything!" Ruthbert responded, furiously tapping at the controls.

"Well then, where is it?"

Ruthbert stopped tapping for a moment. "Err, sorry Gran, force of habit. Just some more puffery. What I meant to say was, no, we don't have any more rope."

"I'll puffery you!" roared Gran in consternation.

While the conversation was going on, Gram had been making her way to where one of the broken ropes dangled over the side.

Gram snapped her fingers. "Your pants, Gran!"

"What?"

"Your pants! We can use your pants! Whip 'em off, buster!"

"I don't think that's exactly decent!"

"Oh you silly man! You're wearing your long johns.

There's hardly a difference!"

"Of course!" Gran unbelted his pants which, it turned out, were much too large to stay up by themselves. They dropped quickly, revealing a set of resplendent rainbow long johns beneath them.

"Toss 'em!" said Gram. Gran picked up his pants and underhanded them to her with the practiced smoothness of a softball pitcher. Gram caught them easily.

"Be careful, Gram!" cried Nia.

Deja couldn't believe her eyes. They were still more than a thousand feet up in the air, in a rapidly disintegrating balloon twisting and turning sickeningly, and her grandma looked like it didn't bother her at all. In fact, *she placed her foot on the side of the basket and then leapt into the air,* grabbing at the small portion of rope still tied to the balloon with one hand while she held Gran's pants in the other.

At the same time, Gran headed towards her, grabbing her at the ankles, pulling her back towards the basket. Gram began to wrap the pants around the rope, tying a knot with incredible nimbleness.

The only way to describe it was that they looked like experts. They looked like this was not their first time trying to repair a damaged balloon, mid-flight, with a pair of trousers.

But that couldn't be true, could it? Deja looked back up at the balloon and turned very cold. One of the remaining five ropes was visibly straining. It would break in moments, and that would just make the other ropes have to work even harder. Ruthbert was right. They weren't going to make it.

The thought made her strangely calm. She put her hand to her stomach and felt the balloon brochure that Rutherford had given her. All three of the children enjoyed reading, but not for the same reasons. Nia read for excitement. She liked wild stories full of wild people with wild problems. Recently, she had started getting into teen romance novels. D'Angelo read for information. His bookshelf at home was full with volumes of maps, diagrams, detailed explanations, and—of course—conspiracy theories.

Deja read for comfort. When she was scared, uncomfortable, or anxious, reading could take her outside of herself for a little while. The words hardly mattered. It was the act of moving her eyes across the letters, sounding out the words, and understanding. Even reading a cereal box or street signs made her feel a little better.

Gram and Gran were now wrestling with the long end of the rope, tying it to the other leg of Gran's trousers, righting the basket a bit as they did so. There was nothing to do. They were going to succeed, or they weren't.

What better time to read?

Deja flipped the brochure open, and her mouth gaped. How had they forgotten?

"Mr. Rugglesford, THE SAFETY FEATURES!"

"What?" Ruthbert asked.

"THE FIVE NEV-R-FAIL SAFETY FEATURES! The balloon has safety features!"

Ruthbert smacked his forehead. "How could I have forgotten? They're right here. But which one? The Anti-Grav Magnet? The Protective Bubble? The Hang-Glider Extension? The CloudHook? The Telescoping Stilts? There's too many choices!"

Deja flipped the brochure to the page announcing the safety features. Next to a photograph of each feature, there was a short description:

> ***The Anti-Grav Magnet:*** *THE MOST TRUSTED SAFETY FEATURE IN USE TODAY!*
> ***The Protective Bubble:*** *ONE HUNDRED PERCENT PROTECTION IN ALL WEATHER CONDITIONS!*
> ***The Hang-Glider Extension:*** *VOTED SAFETY FEA-*

TURE OF THE YEAR BY THE INTERNATIONAL GUILD OF BALLOONISTS!
The CloudHook—

There was a ripping sound behind her.

"Hurry up!" Gran urged Rutherford, "My pants aren't gonna hold out that long!"

Rutherford wailed, "But which to pick?"

The CloudHook: *MADE WITH NATURALLY STRONG MATERIALS FOR A SUPERIOR SAFETY EXPERIENCE!*
The Telescoping Stilts: *#1 SAFETY FEATURE: THE MOST RELIABLE OF METHODS!*

Deja closed the brochure and thought very carefully.

"I know which feature to use, Mr. Ruthbert," she said proudly.

Which feature did Deja suggest to Ruthbert?
If you get stuck, Gram has a hint for you on the next page!

Hint from Gram

It's strange, but true: companies can legally lie to you in advertisements and articles. The legal term really is **puffery**, and the rules are simple:

1. What they **claim** must be so exaggerated that it would be difficult to believe.
2. What they say can't make any specific claims; it can only make general claims of superiority.

Deja knows that when you're looking for puffery, it can help to look for words like "best," "most," and "strongest," which make the product sound superior, as well as descriptions like "famous," "world-renowned," and "trusted," which *sound* like they're claims of quality but don't actually tell you *who* feels that way.

Claims about the quality of a product that give specific information, such as *who* thinks the product is good ("Lisa Dimple loves Tasty-Os!") or *how* the quality was rated ("A 2016 survey found that people enjoy Tasty-Os the best out of five cereal brands") are less likely to be puffery.

So, what about the claims made about the safety features? Which ones seem exaggerated or vague? Which one makes the most specific claim?

Conclusion: Deja Wings It

"The Hang-Glider Extension!" Deja called.

"Righto!" said Ruthbert as he pulled a purple cord coming out of the control panel.

The basket shuddered and two huge, colorful, triangular wings unfolded from the sides with a deafening *WHUMP*. Gram, Gran, and Ruthbert, who weren't strapped in, fell to the floor of the basket. For a second, Deja thought they were in big trouble. As she watched, the basket—which held them—completely detached from the balloon, which sailed away from them with surprising speed, spinning up into the air with its now useless ropes (and one pair of pants) whipping about like the tentacles of an angry octopus.

But the wings held them aloft now, and their descent was considerably slower than before.

"Now what?" asked Gram.

"I don't know," replied Ruthbert. "The way the wind is blowing, we're going to get carried out to sea if we can't find some place to land, and quickly."

"Well, then bring us down!" said Gran.

"It's not that simple. We're very high in the air. If I tried to bring us all the way to ground level with such speed, we'd go into a nosedive and splat right into the ground. If only there was something tall we could land on. Are there any mountains on this island I don't know about?"

"The only mountain on this island is the mountain of lies you told us," grumbled Gran.

Nia was still pale from fright, but her eyes lit up. "There's no mountain, but there *is* a Tower!"

"By gum, you're right, Nia," said Gran. "The Tower, Ruthbert! Land us on the top of the Tower!" And sure enough, the Tower was swinging into view. Deja could even see the chickens pouring out of the henhouse to watch the strange birdlike creature that was heading towards them.

Ruthbert adjusted his hat, which was leaning at a precarious angle. "Easy for you to say, but I need some kind of runway to land, and we don't have one."

"I can handle that!" said Deja. Cupping her hands to her mouth, she called as loudly as she could: "CHICKEN FORMATION ALPHA!"

"Chicken for WHAT?" D'Angelo said.

"CHICKEN FORMATION ALPHA!" Deja yelled again. She put all her breath into it, but the wind was rushing, and she wasn't sure how far her voice was carrying.

Gram stared at her for a moment and then shrugged. "CHICKEN FORMATION ALPHA!" Gram howled.

Now Gran got into it. "CHICKEN FORMATION ALPHA!" he caterwauled.

And as the three of them joined their voices, the chickens stilled and cocked their heads to the sky. Then, in a flurry of movement, they quickly formed two perfect straight lines.

"Incredible!" said Ruthbert. "A chicken landing strip! A bit unorthodox, but I think it'll do."

One thing was for sure: Ruthbert was a skillful pilot. He landed them right between the lines of chickens with surprising gentleness. They scrambled out of the basket. The chickens stared at them in total silence. Gram stared back.

"Chicken formation alpha?" she asked.

Deja explained, "You said you were teaching them to dance, so I figured maybe I could train them to do something too."

"Unbelievable. I'd been at that for months and was starting to think you can't train chickens to do anything other than breakdancing," said Gram.

The chickens continued to stare in silence.

"OK, chickies," Deja said. "End formation!" She clapped her hands, and in a couple of moments, the chickens were back to shuffling around on the rooftop looking for bugs and corn.

"If I hadn't seen it with my own eyes, I wouldn't believe it," said Ruthbert. "I guess some things that sound unbelievable are true. Racecar crab takes the flag, as they say."

Gran had had enough. "Ruthbert, you're the most duplicitous dunderhead in the world! In the universe! In a universe of universes! There's never been a rascal as rascally as you!"

Ruthbert looked down in dismay. "Is that...is that puffery?" he asked.

"No," Gran said firmly. "No, it is not."

Ruthbert hugged him for what seemed like the longest time.

Chapter 11: Gram and Gran Save the Summer, and Also Probably the World

"Ruthbert, NO!" Nia called out with a gasp, as Ruthbert's fingers closed tightly around the lever at the back of the packed newsroom. She could feel the faintest tingle on the back of her neck, like something important was about to happen, something she would never forget.

It seemed most everyone was there: her family, obviously, but also Phineas, the neighborhood kids, and most of the store owners they'd met this summer. (Ms. Ramekin had run over to the commotion so quickly that her apron looked dirty for once.)

Now, all eyes were on Ruthbert, who held in his grasp the fate of the whole country, maybe even the planet. Things had most certainly spiraled out of control. How had this happened?

* * *

The day had started uneventfully enough. Gram and

Gran were having celery tea and rutabaga scones while the kids were taking some time to read in their room. (OK, D'Angelo was watching internet videos, but between each he was researching articles to see if any of them were credible.) Ruthbert was chatting with Gram and Gran gleefully. He'd brought the treats over to apologize for all the mischief he'd caused the past few weeks.

For her part, Nia was savoring the time. In a few days, the kids would be going back to Brooklyn to reunite with Mom, and while Nia looked forward to school and normalcy, she had to admit that the summer had been more special than she'd imagined. Gram and Gran were actually pretty fun, and she'd come to accept their odd ways as part of who they were. Who knew? Maybe there was a part of her that was silly too, somewhere deep, deep down. Nia listened to the conversation across the hall with half an ear:

"So that is why I'm trying to get ice cream banned," proclaimed Ruthbert.

"Surely that's not necessary," said Gram.

"Oh, but it is. I've looked at the data. Every month that more people eat ice cream, there are more shark attacks. So, if we stop eating ice cream, the shark attacks will go down!"

Gram shot Gran a glance. "Figures don't lie, but liars figure" was one of Gran's favorite lines—but even *he* looked like he needed to think this one over. Something about Ruthbert's reasoning was definitely fishy...or sharky.

"Well, while you two discuss, I'll just excuse myself to the bathroom," Ruthbert said.

Gram and Gran fell into a deep conversation. So much so that they didn't notice that Ruthbert wasn't walking toward the bathroom at all. He was heading toward the hatch that led to the computer room.

* * *

"So that's it," Gram had said a few minutes later. "People eat more ice cream in the summer months. And there are probably more shark attacks then because there are more people in the water. We'll have to tell Ruthbert he's all mixed up."

Just then, the lights turned red, and sirens began blaring throughout the apartment. Nia and her siblings rushed into the living room to see what the matter was.

"It's the computer alarm," shouted Gram over the din. "Probably just a false alarm. I doubt someone could get down there. It's top secret."

But Nia already knew who *someone* was. It had to be Ruthbert. That's why he'd taken such an interest in her and Gram and Gran. He'd been trying to get access all summer! But why? What would he want with some dingy computer room, even if it *was* hidden?

"We'll go check it out," said Nia. "I remember the code. We'll be safe, promise."

"Hang on," said Deja. "There has been a secret room this whole summer and I'm just getting to see it now?" She gave her siblings a dirty glance, but her curiosity was too great to slow them down.

"Just call if you need us!" said Gran. "I'm going to see if I can find an override switch for this alarm. I find it much easier to hear when the alarms aren't blaring."

"What?" asked Gram. "I can't hear you because the alarms are blaring!"

The kids rushed to the elevator and Nia entered the code—two zeroes and six ones—and it whirred to life.

* * *

At first, Nia couldn't really tell if the room had been ransacked, since it looked disheveled in the first place. Benji the computer mouse was still there, running furiously on his wheel. But the hatch to the emergency ladder had clearly been broken open. And while there were no alarms sounding down here, the room was now cast in an eerie red glow.

"What is this place?" asked Deja.

"Gram and Gran's computer room," said Nia. "They said they received the code to it when they got the apartment, but to be honest, it just feels like an overstuffed basement to me."

"Still, there's some pretty cool stu—"

"Ahem," said a voice.

"D, was that you?"

"Ahem! It is me, the long-lost Barnaby Babel! No, no—that's no good. It is I, the great and glorious Barnaby Babel. No, no… too much. Ahem. Welcome, dear children.

I'm Barnaby Bab—no, still no good. Could someone help over here?"

By now, the kids could tell the sound was coming from behind a stack of boxes Gran had piled up at the far side of the room. But what shocked them was what they found when they removed them. A giant face flickered on a set of monitors that covered the whole wall. And it appeared to be—for lack of a better word—alive!

"Now, that's more like it. It was getting claustrophobic in here," said the voice.

"Who are you?" asked D'Angelo, forgetting that the voice had already told him his name.

"Barnaby Babel, of course. Builder of this Tower, and former associate of your grandparents."

"You know Gram and Gran?" asked Deja.

"Sure do! Or did. I'm not sure how to describe it, honestly. Gram and Gran were colleagues of mine, once. Like me, they were early believers in the internet. Unlike me, they didn't get trapped inside of it!

"But I can see that it's time for a flashback," he continued. "Once upon a time," he began grandly. "— No, wait. That's no good. Let's try again."

Babel's voice dropped to a wistful whisper. "Now, this is more like it," he intoned, and began to tell the whole story. How he, Gram, and Gran had been colleagues who'd believed the internet was the wave of the future. How they'd worked together on creating electronic marvels until Gram and Gran decided one day that they needed to stop their work and see the world.

"Surely they must have told you they knew me." Babel said, confused.

"They say a lot of stuff," all three children said, wearily, in unison.

"I see. In any case, one day, I was working on some code in Babel Tower, when something went wrong."

"What happened?" D'Angelo asked.

"To be honest, I don't know. Last thing I remember, I was sitting in front of the computer, and then…I lost all track of time and space."

"I know the feeling," Nia interjected.

"And when I regained consciousness, I was here…inside the internet. What had reawakened me, you see, was a little nagging feeling…a feeling that someone, somewhere, was searching—searching for something he was not meant to have. And the feeling wouldn't go away. It was there all the time. Have you ever had a seed caught in your teeth, and you try to get it out with your tongue? It was like that only—errr—without a seed…or a tongue.

"I began to cast my mind this way and that. I stretched it across oceans. I bounced it off satellites. I traced that feeling back to its source and came away with a name: Ruthbert Rugglesford. He was already here, in my Corner, searching for this very room! And since I didn't have a body anymore, I needed someone to watch over this computer room so it never fell into the wrong hands," the voice concluded.

"That's how Gram and Gran got the penthouse!" Nia jumped in, proud that she'd pieced together the mystery. "YOU were the one who sent them the postcard that said they'd won a lottery."

"I needed someone I could trust, and I'd trust your Gram and Gran with my life. But I didn't want anyone to know I was here."

"Why not?" asked Deja.

"It's embarrassing."

"You're basically the internet, Mr. Babel. Why would that be embarrassing?"

"You might think having a consciousness distributed over a vast global network of high-tech relays and connected by a series of standardized communication protocols would be wonderful...but you wouldn't *believe* the things I've seen! People were supposed to use the internet to transmit knowledge, but instead, they used it to transmit *everything*: all the world's knowledge, but all its ignorance too! For instance, did you know that the French diplomat, Charles Maurice de Talleyrand-Périgord, was so afraid of falling out of bed that he wore fourteen nightcaps at the same time?"

"Wow, really?" Nia said.

"I don't know!" Babel wailed. "Is Nuclear Pasta the

strongest material in the universe? Was there a horse-powered boat named *The Experiment*? I don't know! But it's all there—you can look it up!"

D'Angelo was interested in the discussion, but given that the room was still bathed in red light, he sensed there might be something even more interesting at hand. "So what's this?" he said, waving his fingers around the red light.

"Oh, right. Sorry about that," said the voice, and the lights returned to a normal hue. "You see, it appears we are in a bit of a crisis."

* * *

Babel explained that Ruthbert had broken into the computer room's mainframe to insert a new piece of code directly onto the internet, and that this code was so dangerous it could destroy the internet across the entire planet. "I was able to slow him down, but it's only a matter of hours before that code gets out, and if it does… well, that's the end."

"What does it do?" asked Nia.

"It gives its user the power to change the entire internet, to rewrite all online records—even government ones— to say whatever they want. Someone could change the history books to say that they're an Olympic champion, or the 57th president of the United States, or…or…the world's largest cow! You could edit the records so everyone would think Gram was called Gran, and Gran was called Gram! Even the trustworthy sites would be vulnerable to change."

"I dunno," scoffed D'Angelo. "That sounds pretty cool."

"Cool? COOL? Imagine what would happen if that code fell into the wrong hands! We wouldn't know what was real and what was a lie. Governments would topple. People could be convinced into anything, and there'd be nothing we could trust. You'd all end up like me, trapped forever in a web of nonsense! It'd be the collapse of society! A calamity! And, believe me, once the code is out there, it'll be a matter of minutes before someone nefarious grabs it up," Babel said, adding with a wink, "Deja, nefarious means extremely villainous."

Deja nodded.

"OK, OK, sorry," said D'Angelo. "So what do we need to do?"

"I can't stop the code, but I've delayed it. There are three access points to the mainframe throughout town. You have to disable all three access points within an hour of each other. Here, I've marked them on this map." A large map appeared next to Babel's face.

"That's the museum," Nia said, pointing at one of the marked areas.

"And that's behind Le Petit Café." said Deja.

"And that's the cherry orchard." said D'Angelo.

"So that's it? We just have to disable them?" asked Nia.

"Well, no. If he detects you doing this, Ruthbert will try to use the final override lever to get his code out."

"Where did you hide that?" Deja asked.

"In the safest place I know—"

"At the newsroom," came a soft voice from behind the kids. It was Gran, who had slipped into the room with Gram sometime during Babel's speech.

"Hello, my friend," said Gran to the monitor. "I was wondering where you'd gotten yourself to."

"Hello, old chum. It has been far too long," said the monitor screen with a smile. "But, for now, there's no time to lose. If you succeed, there'll be time to catch up later. If not, well, you'll have other problems."

"Kids, you go to the access points. We'll head to the newsroom to try to stop Ruthbert there," said Gram. "And we'll gather as many people from the town to help as possible."

* * *

The computer room had been so dark that the outside world seemed almost unreal, Nia thought, as she squinted her eyes. They had two main problems. They needed to reach each access point, and Deja was still a bit young to go out on her own without at least another kid with her. It's not that Nia didn't trust her sister, but it was her responsibility to keep her safe, and that meant double during a crisis.

But it was just at that moment that a solution presented itself. Across the street, next to a pile of discarded bicycles, were the figures of three kids, all with their faces buried in their phones.

"Duckle! Bugosaurus! Grind_Wizard!" Nia had never

been so happy to see the neighborhood kids in her life, even if they'd been a bit rude in their previous encounters. In one hurried breath, she explained everything.

"It's not that we *believe* you," said Duckle, without looking up.

"It's just that we're bored," said Bugosaurus, also without raising his head.

"Honestly, I'm kinda curious," said Grind_Wizard, a bit sheepishly.

"In any case," said Duckle, "we'll need to split into teams. Grind_Wizard can go with the boy—"

"D'Angelo."

Duckle continued. "Uh-huh. And—"

"I'll go with you!" said Deja. It was clear she was curious about Duckle, and maybe still feeling a little guilty about telling Ruthbert that "Duckle" was her name a few weeks ago.

"I'll go with Bugosaurus, then," said Nia. "We'll rendezvous at the newsroom after we've shut down the access points." It was very clear that Nia was the only person who wanted to put her hands in the middle for a "go team!" But, fortunately, she had enough social savvy to hold off on suggesting it.

"We'll take the orchard. See ya," said Grind_Wizard, as he and D'Angelo made their way to the only location that was likely to have free food.

"We can do the museum," offered Bugosaurus, recalling

that it was where he'd sent Nia earlier.

"Fine, then," said Duckle. "We'll go to the café. I could use a latte, anyhow. Do you need me to define that?" she asked Deja a bit condescendingly.

"Please, I'm from Brooklyn. Do you know what a doppio oat milk green tea dirty chai is?"

Duckle was caught off guard. "A what?"

"It's my mom's favorite order is what it is," said Deja.

"OK, point taken, small fry. Let's go."

* * *

Duckle did wind up having that latte—decaf, of course—as she and Deja searched around for the control panel. They found it in a dingy gray box wired to the back of the building, crudely disguised with a label that read, "Do not tamper." Of course, they tampered.

Inside the box was a small metal plate that said, "Manufactured by the Pulmosan Circuit Corporation, all patents pending. Visit us online for more information on our products." There were a series of wires: a yellow one, a green one, a red one, a blue one, and one striped like a candy cane. A tiny scissor hung from a hook, along with a note:

"Some people are saying the red wire is the thing to cut. But They say that this is usually a trap. Instead, They say the right wire is most often the opposite. Who knows? They say there's no way to check, right? Careful—cutting the wrong wire will lock the system!"

"Why would they put that note in here?" Duckle said suspiciously.

"To be helpful!" Deja said.

Duckle gave Deja a withering side-eye. The side-eye was her most powerful weapon against overconfident people. Her dad once told her that when she was born, the first thing she did was give the doctor the side-eye and the doctor began apologizing immediately.

But Deja smiled sweetly at her.

"People like to be helpful!" Deja said. Duckle sighed and grabbed the clippers.

It only took a second for her to grab them, but in that second, Deja thought for a moment. Something did seem off off about that note.

"Easy," said Duckle. "Green is the opposite of red. Are you ready?"

What did Deja say?
Take a moment to think about the kids' experience this summer, then turn the page when you think you have an idea!

Challenge 1

"Hang on," said Deja. "Just because lots of people say something doesn't mean it's true. We should check this on your phone."

Duckle pulled out her phone and browsed to the Pulmosan Circuit Corporation's site. On it, she found user manuals for their products. A notice read:

"If you ever need to disable one of our systems, we've made it easy to do. Simply cut the candy cane wire and leave the others untouched."

The two gave it a try. The device, which had been purring softly, whirred to a stop. Duckle glanced down at Deja, who was clearly pleased with herself.

"That's pretty clever," she said, giving her a fist bump. "My name's Angela, by the way."

* * *

"So why are we here again?" asked Grind_Wizard, his mouth full of cherries.

"Gotta disable an access panel," D'Angelo replied. His mouth was cherry-free, but only because he'd stuffed them into his pockets, as a snack for later.

"Where would we even find that?"

D'Angelo prided himself on noticing things others did not: the odd spray paint along the sidewalks, the street cameras in Brooklyn, and a mysterious metal hatch in the cherry orchard. "It's no worries. I saw it last time I was here, right… there." D'Angelo pointed at the ground just below Grind_Wizard's feet, where a small metal hatch peeked out from below some dirt and mulch. "Let's open this up."

Inside the hatch were three screens, each with a differently colored button just beneath it: one red, one green, and one blue. A note had been taped to the reverse side of the hatch door. The paper was a bit wrinkled, but it was still legible:

"If nothing is true, then everything is."

Grind_Wizard was not amused. "What's *that* supposed to mean?"

"I'll tell you what it means. It means that something suspicious is going on," said D'Angelo.

"Very," Grind_Wizard agreed.

"Why would someone put a philosophical note in a hidden metal hatch in a cherry orchard?"

"Only one possible explanation: someone or some*thing* wants us to know the truth—the *real* truth—the truth *they* won't tell us." Grind_Wizard said.

"Exactly. And it's up to us to follow the breadcrumbs…"

"…read the signs…"

"…go down the rabbit hole…"

"…pull back the curtain…"

"…expose the hand that's pulling the strings…"

"But what does it mean? If everything is true, nothing is?"

D'Angelo shrugged and looked down at the screens. The

first was colorful and highly ornate, reading "pick red." In small font below, it also read: "Brought to you by Redbutton.com. Visit our site to purchase t-shirts and other swag."

The second screen was equally colorful. It read: "Team Green—endorsed by four out of five psychologists and the American Academy of Astronomers. Greenbutton.org."

The third screen was less interesting. It just said: "Press the blue button for system shutdown. All others will lock you out. Bluebutton.BarnabysCorner.gov."

Grind_Wizard stroked his chin and tried to look thoughtful. "Well, I do like BarnabysCorner.gov—they have useful information, like where the skate parks are located. They've always been reliable in the past, but maybe that's just what they *want* us to think. And if that last screen is right, we only get one guess. How can we know? Maybe we should just mash all three at once and hope for the best."

"That won't be necessary," replied D'Angelo.

Which button will D'Angelo press?
Take a moment to think about the kids' experience this summer, then turn the page when you think you have an idea!

Challenge 2

D'Angelo explained that the note was, in fact, a clue. "It's basically saying that if we don't know what to trust, anything will look believable. I used to think that was true, too, so I only believed the sites in my feed, and I thought all online sources were basically the same.

"But the red and green buttons are clearly fakes. The red button is a commercial site trying to sell us stuff, and the green one, even if this organization *is* legitimate, is backed by people who wouldn't know anything about this system. That leaves us with only one choice," he said.

"Wait, are you *sure* you're right?" Grind_Wizard asked, a tremble in his voice.

"Nah. People who are 100% sure they're right are the easiest to fool," D'Angelo said. "There's no way to be 100% sure about anything. But you can't go around mistrusting everything. If BarnabysCorner.gov has earned your trust in the past, that's good enough for me today. Getting around the internet is all about making smart bets."

"Hardcore," said Grind_Wizard, approvingly.

D'Angelo confidently pressed down on the blue button. The system made a few labored clicking sounds and ground down to a halt.

"That was slick," Grind_Wizard said. "Want a cherry? My name's Keith, by the way."

"Let's get outta here," said D'Angelo, taking the cherry.

* * *

Nia and Bugosaurus raced through the museum, looking for anything that might resemble an access point.

"I can't find it anywhere!" said Nia. "Any luck?"

"Not yet," Bugosaurus said. "And I've been to this museum hundreds of times. I feel like I'd have seen it by now."

Nia admired that Bugosaurus liked the museum as much as she did. *So he was being genuine when he directed her to go visit.* He probably knew quite a bit from his trips. Maybe after all this was over…*Stop*, Nia told her brain. *Think, Nia, think. Focus.* She turned herself back to the task. Something Bugosaurus had said was still rattling in her head.

"Wait, you said you'd been here hundreds of times. So what's the one place you've probably never seen?"

"The back office!" they both said at once. Moments later, they were in front of the final access panel. In it was just a single switch. If it was pressed up, the switch would be set to a zero. If down, it'd be set to a one.

"Ugh," groaned Nia. "Why can't this just say, 'on' or 'off'?" Suddenly, her phone buzzed. It was an email that appeared to be from—wait, was that possible?—the panel.

```
From: AccesssPanel.com.wb

Subject: The Correct Setting
```

Hello! If you're reading this, you've come into close proximity with the internet access panel! Commendations to you on this occasion of joy. It's likely you are shutting it down to protect the internet. We will like to thank you for being a good person.

To turn the panel off, simply flip the switch to "1." Then, when you're finished, we must ask you to fill out a brief survey telling us about you and your experience. As a thank you, you shall be receiving a small cash prize.

All the best,

Team Access Panel

"What a friendly panel!" said Bugosaurus.
"Friendly *and* generous," agreed Nia.
"Well, what should we do?" Bugosaurus asked.

What will Nia do?
Take a moment to think about the kids' experience this summer, then turn the page when you think you have an idea!

Challenge 3

"Something felt off about that email, but I couldn't quite put my finger on it," he said. "You make a good case." Then he blushed. "Before anything happens, in case we're about to collapse civilization, I just wanted to say that my real name is Bradley." *I like that, Nia thought. Bugosaurus—err, Bradley—seems like someone I want to know.*

Nia nodded at Bradley. Bradley nodded at Nia. She flipped the switch to "0" and the machine's faint hum stopped.

* * *

The newsroom buzzed with excitement and stress. Ruthbert, standing at the back wall, had a wild look in his eyes. His fingers curled around a yellow steel lever, the kind that looked like it took a lot of pressure to flip—but also the kind that did something important once pulled. Ruthbert was tugging at it, and it was beginning to budge.

Time was doing something strange. Nia couldn't tell if it was passing very slowly or very quickly. And meanwhile a chorus of voices from the townspeople had erupted in increasingly desperate pleas:

"Stop, Ruthbert!"

"No!"

"Don't do it!"

Gram and Gran had come through—they'd warned so much of the town—and the room was full of people trying to stop Ruthbert.

"Don't come any closer!" he cried. "Or I'll flip the lever!"

There were horrified gasps from the crowd, but Gram shouted, "You're trying to flip the lever anyway, you rapscallion, you miscreant, you jackanapes!"

If Ruthbert had known what those words meant, he might have paused. Instead, he stared around the room. "Don't you see?" he stammered. "All my life I wanted people to respect me, the way you do celebrities and athletes and astronauts. Well, now I can *be* an astronaut. My new program will ensure that! I can make the internet say anything I want! And the best part is, they'll be no way to check! All of the sites will agree! It'll be an internet without conflict."

"But everyone agreeing on something doesn't make it true," shouted D'Angelo. "And once this code is out, anyone can take advantage of it. Anyone can erase what's true and replace it with lies. We won't be able to trust anything online."

Ruthbert huffed and grabbed the lever more tightly. "That's easy for you to say. The internet is already full of lies and falsehoods and fibs. I'm just telling the best one. Thousands of people already think the moon landing was faked, so who cares if I change the facts to make them right? And once I do, people will love me!"

"But it won't be *true*," said Nia. "It'll just be online. That's not reality."

"Close enough," Ruthbert shot back. His hand was still on the lever.

"There was a time," said Gram, "that Gran and I thought we could find ourselves online too. We were there at the beginning, following Barnaby Babel around and believing in his dream, a wild, free internet full of love and good ideas and people helping each other."

"But we got so caught up in that dream," said Gran, "that we forgot to wake up. We didn't notice the people who had gone online just for profit, self-importance, or to trick others.

"And we started spending so much time tending to our lives online that we forgot about the family around us. Our daughter learned that she couldn't rely on us," he said, looking down at his feet. "So we unplugged. We took our savings and decided to travel the world—the *real world*."

Ruthbert sneered, but it wasn't a scary sneer. To Nia, it looked sadder than anything. "I bet the real world was *so much better*," he spat out.

Gram met his sneer with a sad smile. "Ah..." she sighed. "If only that were true. Flitting around the world, living by our wits, seeing sights, and uncovering mysteries was exciting, but it didn't make us feel any more fulfilled."

"We realized that what we were missing wasn't real *things*, or real *places*. It was real *connections* with real *people*. Real *trust*," added Gran. "Real *family*."

"Easy for you to say, Gram. When you were getting

started, there wasn't really an internet. Not like today. There were probably phonographs and telegrams. If a kid decided to bully you, her or his jerk friends saw it and no one else." Ruthbert's hand was starting to shake, but he was still pulling on that lever. "But now everything is online. Everyone sees everything. If someone teases me, the whole world sees—all my friends, all the people I want to become my friends. Do you know what that feels like?" said Ruthbert in a half rage, half sob.

"It's really easy to feel lost," said Nia. "That's why you can't let people online tell you what matters. You have to decide it yourself. People who are happy and having fun don't have time to lie and scam and pick on others anyway. The ones you see online are doing it because they feel small too—and they think the only way for them to feel big is by trying to tear down others around them."

"But they seem so *happy*!" Ruthbert shot back. "All I see are posts with happy, smiling people with perfect memories, like the photos that come with picture frames in the store. Perfect families on perfect days. My photos don't look like that at all. I'm usually blinking. Or looking away. Or it's raining. It's never enough."

"But don't you know those photos in the picture frames are fake?" asked D'Angelo. "Those posts aren't real—or at least they're cherry-picked to make everything look wonderful. Growing up means you know the world is complex, and it's often *not* wonderful, even for the people who claim to have it all. You see them dancing in the rain but miss that their shoes are soaked through. You see them taking photos of their food but they never actually eat it. It's a conspiracy, all right. But it's one we've done to ourselves."

Gran put his hand on D'Angelo's shoulder. The two of them had really grown close since that day in the Great Thinking Chair. "A house built on lies is no home at all," he offered.

"So THEY'RE the villains?" asked Ruthbert.

"They're just people who are trying to make the world feel a little better for themselves. It's understandable, but now you've seen the downside. Sometimes people get so focused on trying to feel better themselves that they do harm to others," said Gran. "And that's all the internet is—just people. It shows the good in us, but it shows the bad in us too. That's why we have to look so carefully for the truth when we're online."

"Ruthbert, I know you're trying so hard to be who you think others will admire," said Gram. "But, deep down, people need to be able to tell what's real and what's not. Because you *aren't* fiction. You're a real person standing right in front of me."

"And you happen to be one of the weirdest, silliest, most hilarious people I've ever met," Nia added.

"But, but…what if that's not enough?"

"Of course it's enough, Ruthbert," said Gram. "The internet can promise us pills to make us tall, or the world's greatest coffee, or any number of things we want to be true. But if we love ourselves enough, we can resist that illusion and look for something more real. I promise you it's out there." She gave Nia's hand a squeeze.

A voice from somewhere distant carried through the air, though no one could be quite sure whose it was. "*You're enough, Ruthbert,*" the voice said in a wistful whisper. "And you always were." The lights flickered a tiny bit.

With that, Deja ran over and gave Ruthbert a tight, teary hug. The yellow lever slipped from his fingers.

"Thank you, Deja," Ruthbert said, closing his eyes. "I'm glad I didn't pull that lever. In some way, I think I was hoping to be stopped. I suppose that's why I left all those weird puzzles at the access points. I figured you all knew enough to solve them."

"Well," Deja said, looking around the room, "we had some great teachers."

At last, Ruthbert wrapped his arms around his friend in return.

"Now," said Gram. "I think we've all earned some extra crispy bacon-jalapeno-cheddar-gorgonzola poppers."

"With grass juice!" shouted Gran.

* * *

A few days later, after a cheerful goodbye, a tugboat ride, and a long bus trip, Barnaby's Corner felt like a far-off dream.

Replacing it was the warm, stuffy smell of Mom's minivan: a mix of air freshener, Cheerios, and home.

"I suppose we *could* invite Gram and Gran for Thanksgiving," Mom said. "And it'd be nice to see Phineas again, if he has any time for us after breaking that big story on Barnaby Babel's contributions to the internet. I wonder how he got *that* scoop!"

"Mr. Paperplate always keeps his nose to the ground," D'Angelo said. "There's news a go-go, as they say."

"I know he's a good reporter, but there's something fishy about that exclusive interview he got. Why did he say Babel was in 'an undisclosed location'? The guy has been missing all these years, and now he won't say where he's been or where he is?"

"He probably doesn't want to give away too much Personally Identifiable Information," Nia responded.

"But—"

"Mom," said Deja, "chill out. Not everything is a conspiracy." She winked at D'Angelo.

D'Angelo jumped in. "So anyway, about Thanksgiving, I think you should invite Gram and Gran…*and* Ruthbert. Mom, you promised."

"Oh, that's right. He's welcome too."

"He promised no more villainy or nefarious acts!" Deja chimed in enthusiastically if a bit unhelpfully. Fortunately, Mom didn't seem to notice.

Nia shifted in her seat. "And don't forget Bugo—I mean, Bradley—is going to be here next weekend with his family. We're going to the Metropolitan Museum of Art."

"Whew," Mom said. "It sounds like you met a ton of people this summer. I'm just glad that Gram and Gran didn't ruin it."

"Ruin it?" asked D'Angelo incredulously. "Gram and Gran basically *saved* the summer!"

Mom was taken aback. D'Angelo hadn't seemed this positive about anything in, well, ever. Maybe her parents really had grown up since she saw them last?

"Well, in the meantime, there are still a few days before school, enough time for the three of you to do some house chores. I was reading an article online just today. Did you know they say that tidying the house is a great way to learn teamwork and discipline?"

"Oh, Mom," Deja said, smacking her hand to her forehead. "Don't you know you can't believe everything you read on the internet?"

THE END

Gram & Gran Save the Summer
Teacher Guide

Dive into thrilling teaching tips and fun ways to invite *Gram and Gran* to your class - just zap the QR code!

Acknowledgements

Steve and Dan would like to thank the myriad people who helped usher this book into the world, starting with Brad and Alaina Weinstein, who – along with the TeacherGoals team – believed in this project and took a chance on it (and us). Thank you for all of your incredible support, counsel, encouragement, and wisdom. We offer our deep gratitude to our illustrator Louis Decrevel, who got to know our characters well enough to shape and sharpen our own vision of them. You made the inhabitants of Barnaby's Corner dance right onto the page. Likewise, we want to thank our thoughtful and fantastic editors: Lois Budesheim, Carrie Turner, Andrew Sobel, and Heather Brown. Each of you helped polish this story until it shined, leaving every draft far better than you found it. Our deep thanks also to Faith Rogow for sharing thoughtful feedback on our draft.

Steve wants to thank Charell, the love of his life, who was an early advocate for this text and the work it took to complete it. Your spark is so darned bright that it lights up everyone around you. He'd also like to thank his son Cole—for whom he wrote this book—who showed him that there is no upper limit on love. He offers deep gratitude to his parents and brother for being the kind of people who love literacy and technology and never pressured him to choose one or the other. Additionally, Steve wishes to honor his colleagues at Uncommon Schools, who have coached and nurtured him for well over a decade, as well as the many mentors, professors, peers, teachers, and friends who have encouraged him as a writer and educator. There isn't nearly enough space here to name you all here, but if you're reading this – yes, I'm talking about you. Finally, he'd like to thank his students, with a special shout out to his journalism students (the writers and editors at *The Student Voice* and *The Messenger*) who reminded him – and remind him still – that a better world needs and is worth fighting for.

Dan wants to thank Deva and Rosemary for their constant support, advice, patience, and good humor (I wrote a booooook!); Mom, Dad, and Elena for their encouragement; the Lifeboat Crew, who followed this project from the beginning, especially Dani Grant and Stacey Lane who saw early drafts; Ann Payne and Christina Ketchem for advice along the way. I have benefited from many wonderful teachers in my life and would especially like to acknowledge Ms. Milligan, for giving me my first chance to share my stories with others, and Professors Nancy Willard at Vassar and Teresa Michals at George Mason University who took my love of children's literature and inspired me to do something with it.

About the Authors and Illustrator

Stephen Chiger and Daniel Pereira are long-time friends who began writing a book together when they were in high school. You know how life goes: one minute you're consuming Mountain Dew in your buddy's basement, and the next thing you know it's *Work! Responsibilities! A Family of Your Own!* A few decades later, they were ready to complete the project, now as award-winning educators with four decades of experience teaching and leading English, journalism, and media.

Steve was the 2015 New Jersey Council of Teachers of English Teacher of the Year and formerly led the Hugh N. Boyd Journalism Diversity Workshop and the Garden State Scholastic Press Association. Having won multiple recognitions for his work in education, he's also the co-author of *Love and Literacy*, a book on 5-12 English pedagogy. Currently a director of literacy for Uncommon Schools, Stephen has a master's in new media journalism from Northwestern University and in educational leadership from Columbia University. He lives in Maplewood, NJ with his wife and son. Find him online at stevechiger.com.

Dan received the 2008 Washington Post Agnes Meyer Teacher of the Year award and is a published author in the field of critical studies in children's literature. He's currently pursuing a master's in social work at George Mason University and holds another in English from the University of Maryland. By the time you read this, he will probably be a therapist working in private practice in the Northern Virginia area. He lives in Alexandria with his wife, daughter, and two indescribable cats.

Louis Decrevel lives in South Australia with his wife and children. His award-winning writing and illustrations have appeared in national and international publications, in corporate branding, and in projects for the Australian Government. He received his Master's degree at the University of South Australia, with a thesis called *Word and Picture at Play*. But what he really enjoys is writing silly stories, drawing funny pictures, and playing and exploring with his kids. You can find him at Loueee.com.

More Children's Books
from

Peter O'Meter

By Tricia Fuglestad

Peter O'Meter is an interactive book that explores the emotional journey of a young robot named Peter. With an upgraded eMotion panel that needs calibration, readers can help Peter identify his feelings as he navigates his retro-futuristic world. This book offers interactivity and augmented reality to enhance the reading experience, allowing  readers to interact with a 3D Peter, make decisions, and communicate their advice. Augmented reality animations bring the illustrations to life, creating an emotive and moving narrative.